Online Research

RESEARCH METHODS

Online Research

TRISTRAM HOOLEY AND RACHEL BUCHANAN

BLOOMSBURY ACADEMIC
LONDON · NEW YORK · OXFORD · NEW DELHI · SYDNEY

BLOOMSBURY ACADEMIC
Bloomsbury Publishing Plc
50 Bedford Square, London, WC1B 3DP, UK
1385 Broadway, New York, NY 10018, USA
29 Earlsfort Terrace, Dublin 2, Ireland

BLOOMSBURY, BLOOMSBURY ACADEMIC and the Diana logo are trademarks
of Bloomsbury Publishing Plc

First published in Great Britain 2012
This edition published 2024

Series design: Charlotte James
Cover image © shuoshu/iStock

A catalogue record for this book is available from the British Library.

A catalog record for this book is available from the Library of Congress.

ISBN: HB: 978-1-3503-1908-0
PB: 978-1-3503-1909-7
ePDF: 978-1-3503-1910-3
eBook: 978-1-3503-1911-0

Series: Bloomsbury Research Methods

Typeset by Deanta Global Publishing Services, Chennai, India
Printed and bound in Great Britain

CONTENTS

SERIES EDITOR FOREWORD

The idea behind this series is a simple one: to provide concise and accessible overviews of a range of frequently used research methods and of current issues in research methodology. Books in the series have been written by experts in their fields with a brief to write about their subject for a broad audience, who are assumed to be interested but not necessarily to have any prior knowledge. The series is a natural outgrowth of the 'What is?' strand at Economic and Social Research Council Research Methods Festivals which have proved popular both at the festivals themselves and subsequently as a resource on the website of the ESRC National Centre for Research Methods.

Methodological innovation is the order of the day, and the 'What is?' format allows researchers who are new to a field to gain an insight into its key features, while also providing a useful update on recent developments for people who have had some prior acquaintance with it. All readers should find it helpful to be taken through the discussion of key terms, the history of how the method or methodological issue has developed, and the assessment of the strengths and possible weaknesses of the approach through analysis of illustrative examples.

In this book, *Online Research*, Tristram Hooley and Rachel Buchanan offer an updated discussion of conducting research online. This is a timely book given the ongoing interest among social science researchers on how to engage in such research in methodologically grounded and innovative ways.

The first edition of the book, titled *What is Online Research?*, was published in 2012, and since that time new technologies have emerged with increasing pace, and digital methods have been developed to both harness the value of new data sources and to explore the emerging digital society. However, Hooley and Buchanan emphasize that there remains continuity between what was known decade(s) ago and today about online research practices. In fact, they encourage readers to engage fully with the 'older' literature on online research, as much of it holds true today. Moreover, in the book, they highlight how the broader methodological landscape is relevant to the social scientist engaged in online research. That is, what a social science researcher needs to know about survey design or conducting an ethnography is relevant to engaging in thoughtful online research. They emphasize that an online researcher must learn to balance what is known about onsite research methods when working in an online context. Indeed, there book offers critical guidance on how to do just this.

Across the nine chapters of the book, Hooley and Buchanan detail how different methodologies might be 'translated' for an online context. Specifically, they discuss surveys, interviews and focus groups, ethnographies and experiments, offering updated examples of what it might looks like to conduct online research using these methods. They then introduce readers to critical considerations related to the nature of online data and ethics of online research, while also illustrating how the online context might be best used to communicate research findings.

This book contributes core knowledge on a contemporary topic of great interest in social sciences. Interdisciplinary scholars across research paradigms will find this book particularly relevant and central to their understanding of how to carry out online research.

Jessica Nina Lester and Mark Elliot
Series editors

PREFACE TO THE SECOND EDITION

In 2022 Tristram Hooley was contacted by Bloomsbury to ask if he would produce a second edition of the 2012 book *What is Online Research?* On taking it off the shelf and re-reading it, it became very apparent that this could not be a normal second edition. A decade now separated current practice in online research methods from the ideas and advice set out in the first edition. Many of the principles of doing high-quality online social research remained the same, but the context had radically shifted. A second edition was going to require a complete rewrite.

Tristram approached Rachel Buchanan and invited her to collaborate on the second edition. The decision was taken to largely preserve the existing structure of the book, with the addition of two completely new chapters; Chapter 2 which explores the nature of online data and Chapter 8 which examines how researchers can use the internet to communicate their research to others.

The existing chapters that remained from the first edition provided a useful stimulus for thinking about the key issues but in most cases have been completely rewritten. In general, the book avoids relying on material that was available at the time of the first edition in order to provide an up-to-date, state of the art in the field. New methodological writing, analysis and case studies were identified and pre-2012 material was only used where it was seminal or of important historical interest.

Each chapter follows a similar structure, beginning with an introduction to the issues discussed, followed by a case study illustrating what this particular method or issue looks like in practice. The chapter then moves on to look at key issues, challenges and dilemmas, before summarizing the chapter and setting out areas for further reading.

The book is designed as an introductory text for online social researchers. It provides a discussion of the nature of data, ethics and research communication, and it offers chapters focusing on surveys, qualitative methods, ethnographies and experiments. It then provides a discussion of where the field might move in the future. The book offers considerable methodological breadth and encourages researchers to consider the value that mixed-methods, mixed-mode and interdisciplinary research may offer, as well as providing a grounding in the field.

We hope that you enjoy it and find it useful.

ACKNOWLEDGEMENTS

This book has emerged from twenty years of research and engagement with online research methods. It has its origins in the *Exploring Online Research Methods in a Virtual Training Environment* project funded by the Economic and Social Research Council (ESRC) between 2004 and 2006 and TRI-ORM which ran between 2007 and 2009 and which was also funded by the ESRC. We are grateful to Clare Madge, Henrietta O'Connor, Jane Wellens, Julia Meek and Rob Shaw for their pioneering work on these projects. Information about these projects has been archived at https://www.restore.ac.uk/orm/site/home.php

We are also grateful to John Marriott and Jane Wellens who co-wrote the first edition of *What is Online Research?* with Tristram in 2012. Their ideas and insights have continued to inform the new edition.

We would also like to thank our families, universities and Bloomsbury for the support that they have given us in writing this book. It takes a village . . .

CHAPTER ONE

Introduction

Online research methods for a digital world

In 2020 the Philippine-American singer Bella Poarch recorded a ten-second video on the Chinese-owned social media app TikTok in which she bobs her head and pulls faces while miming to the words of the song *M to the B* by the British artist Millie B (a purveyor of the highly niche and culturally specific genre of Blackpool Grime). This proved to be one of TikTok's most popular videos of the year and has been viewed by over half a billion people who have then responded to it by liking it (61 million times), sharing it (42 million times) and leaving 2.2 million comments on it (Jennings, 2020; Poarch, 2020). This tiny intertextual piece of content was a global cultural phenomenon, but what was it, what did it mean and most importantly for this book, how can we study it?

We can of course understand TikTok in a variety of ways. On one level it is a business which sells audience to companies that want to sell their products; on another it is a community of (mainly young) creators riffing off each other, sharing ideas and information, and on another still it is an enormous repository of cultural artefacts. So, what was the point of Bella Poarch's video, who benefitted from it, what does it say about the permeability of culture in a globalized and digitalized world and does all this content flicking across the screens of our phones change the way we behave beyond our immediate interactions with TikTok. These are all potential subjects for social research and raise big questions about how we investigate these kinds of phenomena.

In an investigation of the use of TikTok by young people in Taiwan, Liao et al. (2022) surveyed TikTok users and then linked their survey data to information contained in their TikTok profiles gathered through data mining techniques. This provided a data set that could be analysed to review their demographics, online behaviours and motivations. In another study Li et al. (2021) used content analysis to analyse 331 TikTok videos published by public health agencies during the Covid-19 pandemic. They concluded that the app had considerable public health applications and that public health videos were most effective when they included an element of dance. In the Netherlands, De Leyn et al. (2022) interviewed ten young people between the ages of eight and twelve (tweens) to explore their use of TikTok. They used Jørgensen's (2016) 'media go-along' approach whereby participants provide interviewers with a verbal and visual tour of their media use during the interview. De Leyn et al.'s work provided insights into what young people are watching and why and showed some disjuncture between their use of the technology and their parents' understanding and regulation of it.

As these examples show, online research is highly varied, even when we view it through the lens of a single technology. As new technologies emerge, social researchers have viewed them as both objects of study and as mechanisms for finding out about the social world. However, in this book we reject the idea that the technology begets methodology in any simple and straightforward way and instead seek to detail the inter-relationships between technologies, social forms and the methodologies that researchers use to investigate them.

Online research investigates the online world, but it also explores the intersection and integration of the online with the onsite. We can use online methods to examine both online and onsite phenomena, and similarly we can use onsite methods to examine both the online and the onsite. Increasingly we are using a blend of methods to investigate a blended social reality in which the demarcation between the online and the offline are often very blurred. As the examples above show online research methods range from a researcher sitting next to a young person and having them point at their phone while they talk, to data mining user accounts and integrating that data with survey data. As we go through this book, we will show you many more approaches and possibilities, explore their various advantages and disadvantages and consider how they might be used in practice.

Four decades of methodological development

This book is building on four decades of methodological development. The development of new technologies and new socio-technological formations frames and shapes the nature of online research methods, but it does not mean that online research methods must be rebuilt from scratch every year as technologies change. This book is an updated version of *What is Online Research?* (Hooley et al., 2012) and while very few of the research studies cited or the examples of research practice survived from the previous edition into this, many of the principles of effective practice and the overall categorization of research methods remain valid.

The fact that there is a level of continuity between online research methods over a ten- or even over a forty-year period speaks to the fact that online research methods are part of an even longer tradition of social science methodologies. As you will see, the online researcher does not abandon all the learning from wider methodological work; a survey remains a survey when it is placed online and key issues about recruitment, sampling, analysis and so on remain critical. However, the shift online does result in a shift of context, of participant expectation and in the opening of new possibilities for research. In many ways the principal theme of this book is how the online researcher balances these issues of change and continuity, considering what is the same as in onsite research methods and what varies.

The methodologies that a researcher might use to investigate TikTok are shaped in response to the technology (what TikTok allows users to do, what data it collects and facilitates researchers to access), and the social aspects of using the app (why people use TikTok and what kind of interactions they have). However, online research methods are also shaped by existing onsite research methods, because of this, the core of this book has been organized around four chapters which detail how different methodologies are translated and reframed for the online environment: surveys in

Chapter 4; interviews and focus groups in Chapter 5; ethnographies in Chapter 6; and experiments in Chapter 7. Online research methodologies therefore describe the approaches that researchers take, rather than the tools that they use.

In the revision of this book, we have sought contemporary examples where this is possible. If you want to look further into the history of the field, you can always go back to the first edition. But we also want to illustrate that there is still much to learn from older research which wrestled with the issues that online researchers continue to address and from reflecting on what has changed and stayed the same.

In 1999, Beaudouin and Velkovska (1999) introduced 'the Cyberians' an online community made up of users of a French internet service provider. Beaudouin and Velkovska analysed over 5,000 messages posted on message boards, looked at the way individuals presented themselves on their homepages, interviewed eight of the Cyberians and received survey responses from an additional forty-two. Their main questions were whether it was possible to describe the Cyberians as a community and, if so, what kind of community could exist made up of people who might never speak, touch, make eye contact or meet?

Beaudouin and Velkovska concluded that the Cyberians did constitute a community and noted that a new raft of research would be needed to understand this 'quickly expanding new social universe' (Beaudouin & Velkovska, 1999, p. 109). The online experience of community, which Beaudouin and Velkovska find in Cyberia, has now become a commonplace reality for millions, possibly even billions, of web users across the world. What has changed is the technology which mediates these communities. With these changes come shifts in the affordances of new technologies which in turn shape the way in which community can be enacted. Cyberia looked very different from existing face-to-face communities, but we would argue that Bella Poarch miming to Millie B and 2.2 million people commenting on this is just as far away from the messages being exchanged in Cyberia. Once again, we are faced with questions about whether such a phenomenon can be thought of as a community and what such a community is. Ultimately the only way to answer this question is through research where we seek to establish what is happening, what meaning people place on it, and how it changes their thinking and behaviour.

The online community of the Cyberians was novel because it was comprised of people who did not know each other in their everyday onsite lives. In a way the surprising thing about Bella Poarch's engagement with Millie B is similar. *M to the B* is lifted out of its local context in Blackpool (UK) and afforded new meaning in the globalized community of TikTok. Such interactions are commonplace, but they may not be typical. Evidence shows that the nature of online relationships is shaped by geographic distance, with closer online ties typically related to geographic proximity (Laniado et al., 2018). For many people, digital social networks do not foster the creation of an alternative online community but rather support the building and maintenance of face-to-face relationships. Such blended realities perhaps suggest the need for hybrid research methods, capable of addressing and exploring the simultaneous online and onsite lived reality of individuals.

The porous nature of online spaces also increases our confidence that online research methods do not need to be preserved solely for the investigation of digital phenomenon. When we research online, we are researching real people, participating in real social environments and the fact that the research or elements of their experience are mediated by digital tools and that we may not be proximate to them, does nothing to diminish this reality. Of course, the internet also increases the potential for deception, identify fraud and the adoption of personae, but such phenomena also provide a rich seam of possibilities for researchers (Chiluwa & Samoilenko, 2019).

It is also worth noting that researchers are not just dispassionate observers sitting outside of online spaces and communities. As we discuss in Chapter 8 a key element of using online technologies in research is thinking about how you will participate in such communities and spaces and make use of them to engage participants, tell people about your research, and to move your own career and reputation forward.

More devices than people

The current generation of internet users are using an ever-expanding array of devices to connect to the internet. These include desktop and laptop devices, tablets, phones, televisions and gaming consoles. But it also includes other objects and devices (such as fitness trackers, refrigerators and traffic lights), connected to the internet in a range of different ways. This is sometimes called 'the Internet of Things' and includes different ways in which physical objects can be known to, organized through and connected with the internet. Current estimates put the number of devices connected to the internet over 13 billion and project that this number will double over the next five years (G., 2023). This means that there are now more internet-enabled devices than people and that the collection and organization of data about us is often beyond our knowledge and out of our control.

The growth of devices is accelerating the integration between the online and onsite world. Whether it is checking your phone when you wake up, patching someone in from another location into a face-to-face meeting using Teams or receiving advertisements based on your location, our physical and digital worlds are increasingly intertwined. Even when we manage to put our phones down, we may still be generating data based on the way that we are working out, using our domestic appliances, interacting with public services, gaining qualifications, paying taxes and shopping both online and on the high street. There is a spy in our telephone, in our coffee machine and in the surveillance cameras on the street, but there is also a spy in the devices of others in the crowd which are all collectively gathering, sharing and organizing data about the social world (Tyagi & Shamila, 2019).

The transformation of an increasing amount of human experience into recordable and accessible (or in many cases enclosable) data, clearly offers major opportunities for researchers, but it also presents significant ethical and legal issues that researchers will need to deal with. What is private and what is public is no longer clear, nor is it clear who has the legal right to consent to the use of personal data in a world where proprietary software companies own and sell enormous repositories of individuals' personal data (Zuboff, 2019). Add onto this that much online activity exists under multi-jurisdictional regulation and that most states struggle to enforce regulations in relation to the internet.

We explore these issues in Chapter 2 which looks at the nature of online data in the contemporary world and asks what possibilities trends like big data and the Internet of Things (IOT) offer us. We also pick up many of these issues in Chapter 3 which looks at the ethical issues and reminds us that just because it has become possible to access vast amounts of information and to use this to find out a great deal about individuals and the social world; it does not always mean that we should gather, analyse and publish with such data.

About the book

This book discusses a wide range of methodological traditions and explores how they have been translated into online methods. Because of this broad approach each of the chapters is aimed at a non-specialist audience. While it does not attempt to provide a basic grounding in social science research, suggestions are made of texts that can provide this grounding in each of the areas. The book also provides a glossary, to assist with the technical terminology that the online researcher is required to master.

One of the biggest challenges in working with online research methods is that none of the methods has developed within disciplinary silos. Researchers in education, sociology, geography, psychology, economics and many other disciplines have been re-conceptualizing their approaches and have been exploring how their methodological paradigms are reshaped using online tools. In many cases this has led to creative interdisciplinary cross-fertilization; however, this eclecticism can make the literatures difficult to access. Furthermore, it can present those attempting to synthesize the literature with an additional challenge of negotiating different epistemologies.

This book reflects this interdisciplinarity and draws on a broad review of literatures in relevant disciplines without trying to resolve difference or privilege any particular approach. It does not claim to be a comprehensive literature review but rather to provide an introductory text that is strongly grounded in published academic work from a range of disciplines. There are lots of other excellent books that deal with the subject of online research methods; however, relatively few books have as broad an outlook as this volume.

The speed of change in online technologies and methods means that there is considerable value in revisiting these issues regularly to explore how changes have reshaped methodological practices. This book therefore provides an up-to-date, comprehensive, multidisciplinary work that maps the field of online research methods within the context of a rapidly changing technological landscape.

It is important to note that online research methods cover a far wider set of approaches and strategies than the current volume can hope to address. In this edition we have added a new chapter looking at the nature of online data (Chapter 2), which provides some space to look at big data analysis and data mining, but it would be possible to say more about this (see Attewell et al., 2015 for a starting point). There are also a range of other areas that we could have devoted more space or even whole chapters to, had space allowed, such as online content analysis including the use of AI in this analysis (Lewis et al., 2013; Popping, 2017), online network analysis (Batrinca & Treleaven, 2015; Knoke & Yang, 2019), and usability and ergonomics (Martins et al., 2015). It would also have been possible to say more about key cross-cutting themes and approaches in online research such as gamification, data visualization, integration with analysis software and the use of AI. Many of these issues are touched upon in the subsequent chapters including Chapter 9 where we look forward at the technologies and trends that are likely to shape the future of online research methods.

The book is made up of nine chapters, a glossary and a reference list. The introduction is the first of these and has hopefully set out some of the key issues and the terrain that we are going to travel. In Chapter 2 we look at the nature of online data and then in Chapter 3 move on to explore ethical issues.

The subsequent four chapters focus on different methodological traditions and their translation into the online environment. So, Chapter 4 looks at online surveys, Chapter 5 at qualitative research, primarily through the lens of interviews and focus groups, Chapter 6 at ethnographies and Chapter 7 at experiments. In each of these chapters we map the key methodological issues associated with that approach, consider how these are changed through the move to online and think about how researchers can operationalize the different approaches.

In Chapter 8 we go on to look at how researchers can use the internet to communicate their research and in Chapter 9 explore what the future may hold. We also hope that you will find the glossary useful and believe that the bibliography stands as an invaluable tool, providing a contemporary summary of the state of the art in the field.

The book is designed to be read as a whole; we recognize that many people will dip into chapters as they embark on a particular project. However, while online research methods must be understood as multi-faceted, there are challenges that are faced by all methodological approaches online. Because of this there is a considerable amount of cross-referral between chapters, and the online researcher will gain something by exploring the lessons that have been learnt in different methodological traditions. It is hoped that this volume can provide new online researchers with insights about how to go about undertaking online research. It aims to offer practical solutions, without pretending that there is a one-size-fits-all approach. It is also hoped that it can play a role in the cross-fertilization of ideas across different disciplines and methodological traditions. In a world populated by TikTokers and Cyberians, it could be argued that online research methods are too important to ignore.

Further reading

There is a wealth of good writing about current developments in technology and the internet. Good starting points include *Internet for the people* (Tarnoff, 2022) which looks at issues of ownership and control, Bernal's (2020) *What do we know and what should we do about internet privacy* and *Social media: A critical introduction* (Fuchs, 2021). As we have argued, it is becoming increasingly difficult to separate out internet culture from wider society and culture. Almost all issues now have a digital angle from war, to elections, to careers and leisure. We would recommend that you read widely around all these subjects to help you to gain a more sophisticated understanding of the interaction between society and internet technologies. There are also several other introductions to the area of online research methods which may be helpful in supplementing this book, which we refer to throughout this volume.

Exploring online data

This chapter addresses what data on the internet is and what purposes social researchers can put this to. It provides an introductory description of the internet and the key features of interest to social researchers, before outlining differing ways that online data is described (naturally occurring, big, small, thick, etc.) and exploring issues to consider. The chapter concludes with a summary of key data gathering and analysis techniques.

Research which approaches online data and seeks to use it to understand social phenomena builds on a range of disciplinary traditions, many of which are discussed in more detail elsewhere in this book. An important tradition, particularly when looking at naturally occurring data, is the analysis of media and communications. We would suggest reviewing texts like *Researching communication* (Deacon et al., 2021) and *A handbook of media and communication research* (Jensen, 2020) for an introduction to this tradition. For a more in-depth exploration of research using online data see *Understanding research in the digital age* (Reynolds & Quinton, 2018), *Bit by bit: Social research in the digital age* (Salganik, 2019), *Digital sociology* (Lupton, 2015) or *What is digital sociology?* (Selwyn, 2018).

Case study: Gambling among online casino gamblers before and during the Covid-19 pandemic

To investigate the impact of the pandemic on the behaviour of gamblers in Sweden, Auer and Griffiths (2022) used behavioural tracking data from user accounts to analyse online casino gambling. Auer and Griffiths were given access to the behavioural tracking data of a representative sample of 133,286 Swedish online gamblers by a European online gambling operator. The researchers did not track individual gamblers, but instead they analysed the totality of daily online casino gambling occurring between January and May 2020.

Auer and Griffiths used the behavioural tracking tool *mentor*. *Mentor* uses behaviours such as chasing losses, failed deposits, deposits within sessions, long playing sessions and other criteria to classify players into high-, medium- or low-risk categories. To identify significant changes within the respective time period, the researchers used the Mann-Kendall Test (Yue et al., 2002).

Results showed that while the number of active online gamblers significantly increased over time, the mean average daily bet by online casino gamblers daily significantly decreased over time. Their results indicated that, contrary to public commentary suggesting problem gambling would worsen during the pandemic (due to increased time spent at home), gambling intensity decreased among Swedish online gamblers. Their study varied from other contemporary research into online gambling because they were able to analyse tracking data rather than having to rely on self-report data (self-report data in gambling studies is prone to poor memory recall and social desirability bias) (Auer & Griffiths, 2022).

Issues highlighted

Auer and Griffiths's study indicates that behavioural tracking data provides accurate data compared to data generated through self-report. Given that much online activity is trackable and traceable, detailed and accurate accounts of human behaviour can be produced by analysis of such data.

Access to online data

Auer and Griffiths were not using publicly accessible data, the data used in this study was provided to the researchers by an online gambling company. Much online content is increasingly controlled by a few companies (e.g. Google, Apple, Facebook, Amazon and Microsoft). The increasingly proprietary nature of the internet has led to 'a process whereby a small number of internet companies are said to be replacing the shared technical protocols that have defined the internet for decades with proprietary interfaces and standards of their own' (Winseck, 2020, p. 242). This process of digital enclosure shifts ownership of online spaces to proprietary organizations and has implications for researchers studying online activity. Researchers need to develop strategies for accessing online data.

Limitations and constraints

Auer and Griffith note that their study 'comprised secondary data analysis' (2022, p. 1725). The study was based upon data that had been collected for purposes other than their research and therefore differed to what they might have chosen to collect. The data they used was based on the activity of accounts held with online casinos – an account might be shared among users, potentially distorting the data. The data comprised cross-sectional daily data rather than individually tracking each online gambler. This may have affected the analysis as those gambling at a specific percentile at one time may not have been the same individuals at that percentile at another time. In designing their analysis, Auer and Griffith's research was shaped by the data that they were given access to. Much online data is naturally occurring, rather than researcher elicited, and this affects the research – the implications of this are explored later in this chapter.

What is the internet?

The internet has been described as 'the world's most popular computer network' (Lee, 2014), or a 'network of networks' (Chopra et al., 2019, p. 135). It is a globally connected decentralized network of billions of computers and other devices. Users are connected to the internet when they go 'online'.

The internet is largely made up of three parts:

1. The '*last mile*' refers to the part of the internet that connects the devices in homes, schools and businesses to the internet. This includes the towers that allow people to connect to the internet using their mobile phones.

2. *Data centres* are warehouses that store the many servers that store data and host online applications and web content. Many data centres are owned by companies such as Google and Facebook while others are owned by commercial enterprises that service smaller websites and other companies. Data centres can be anywhere in the world but are often located in remote locations where land and electricity are cheap.

3. The '*backbone*' is the long-distance networks, largely made up of fibre optics, that connect and carry data between data centres and consumers.

Internet social research is undertaken on users' online activity on internet applications such as the web rather than on the physical structures that make up the global network of the internet.

The world wide web

While 'the web' is often used synonymously with the internet, the world wide web is one of many internet applications. Other internet applications include email and BitTorrent (a distributed peer-to-peer file sharing system). The world wide web is a popular and accessible way to publish information on the internet and allows access through web browsers to the websites that make it up. The web is comprised of three layers:

1. The *surface web* is where the content is indexed and assessed by search engines such as Google and Bing. The surface web is the public facing pages of the web.

2. The *deep web* is made up of encrypted information that is not searchable, however users who know the URL of the

sites they seek can access the deep web using standard web browsers.

3. The *dark web*, like the deep web, is encrypted and not searchable; however, access to the dark web requires the use of specialist anonymous browsers (such as Tor) and decryption keys. The dark web began as a channel for anonymous communication and has a reputation of use for illegitimate activity by hackers and criminals; however, there are numerous legitimate uses of the dark web such as by law enforcement agencies or by activists in regions where free speech isn't protected. The primary use of the dark web is for e-commerce – by using cryptocurrency users can make purchases without revealing their identity (Mirea et al., 2019).

The cloud

In discussion of the internet, references to 'the cloud' are a shorthand way of referring to cloud computing. 'Cloud computing' is the delivery of computing services such as databases, networks, software, data storage, analytics and intelligence, over the internet. Users typically only pay for the services they use in a subscription-based consumption and delivery model of IT services. It is a cost-effective model as users do not need to invest in on-premises data storage, IT infrastructure and IT management. Cloud computing is increasingly being used by researchers for purposes such as:

- Data sharing, storage, and analysis: large amounts of data can be stored in cloud storage, which can be accessed and analysed by team members from anywhere;

- High performance computing: it allows researchers to access resources to perform complex calculations and simulations without having to purchase specialist equipment; and

- Machine learning and artificial intelligence: cloud-based machine learning and AI services can be used to scrape and analyse data.

The Internet of Things

The Internet of Things [IOT] represents an extension in internet usage from primarily human-to-human communication to the addition of machine-to-machine communication (Chopra et al., 2019). IOT refers to a rapidly growing network of physical objects ('smart devices') that are connected to the internet with the ability to communicate information collected from sensors, electronics and software to allow for automated decision-making, collection and sharing of data. IOT includes:

- everyday items such as thermostats, appliances, toys, cars and wearables;

- more specialized tools such as industrial and farming equipment, medical devices and satellites; and

- infrastructure such as traffic lights and water systems.

Social researchers can use IOT technology to study human behaviour, human-technology interactions and the impact of technology on societies.

Social media

Websites and mobile applications that enable social networking are referred to as social media. Social media differs from other web content in that social media users participate in the creation of content (Ghani et al., 2019). Social media allows users to connect via platforms where they can create personal profiles, share information, images, videos and communicate with others on the platform.

Different forms of social media have different emphases: Facebook allows for connection with family and friends, shared interest groups and communities; Instagram allows users to share videos and images; LinkedIn is for connection among professional contacts; and TikTok is a platform where users share short videos, usually set to music. Each of these platforms attracts a different mix of users and has seen the emergence of different cultures, ways of interacting and norms. While these are related to the affordances of the platforms, they are not wholly determined by them.

As social media encompasses communication, entertainment, news, networking and marketing, it is a rich source of information for researchers. Social media allows for varied forms of analysis and research such as: social network analysis, sentiment analysis, opinion mining, behavioural research, marketing and advertising research, political science research and for the study of human-computer interaction.

Online data

Data generated by online activities are multiple and varied. There are different ways of conceptualizing this data (naturally occurring, big, small, thick, lively, etc.). Online data (of any type) is not neutral – it has been generated for a specific purpose, the codes used to create data sets and algorithms are always the result of particular questions being asked or commercial problems being solved (Beer, 2017; Youtie et al., 2017). While the same can be said about non-digital data, the original purposes, intent and authenticity of digital data are often opaque.

Naturally occurring data

One reason that the internet is so interesting to social research is the abundance of naturally occurring data. Naturally occurring data differs from manufactured or elicited research data. The latter are generated for the purposes of a specific research study (such as interview or questionnaire responses), whereas naturally occurring data are data that exists independently of and without the researcher (Golato, 2017). Manufactured data allows researchers to control or limit the data that is generated for their study. While disciplines such as anthropology have long favoured the use of naturally occurring data in ethnographic and observational research, disciplines such as psychology have largely depended on elicited data.

For researchers in media and communications, the existence of this vast expanse of online content is an object of study in itself (Webb, 2017). The creation of everything from individual tweets to websites, apps and the internet itself is a phenomenon worthy of study and one which can be approached in a variety of ways which variously could investigate the medium, the message or the place of the content within wider social systems and systems of discourse.

Internet users' online activity leaves digital traces (Thatcher, 2014). These digital traces are a source of naturally occurring data and are the data generated through interaction with digital technologies including browsing history, search queries, social media posts, emails and text messages as well as the data generated by IOT devices such as location data from smart phones and activity data from wearable devices. Naturally occurring online data is produced from almost the entire gamut of human life and interactions (Reynolds & Quinton, 2018) and can take the form of: website links; online discussions; logs of group interactions; images and image tags; financial transaction histories; videos posted online; interactions, trends and hashtags on social media; geospatial information; patents; product sales; consumer reviews; performance in sporting events; dialect maps; citations and more (Goldstone & Lupyan, 2016; Reynolds & Quinton, 2018). Naturally occurring data has been used to gain insight into varied phenomena such as to measure the response of spending to income (Gelman et al., 2014), to study social influence online (Cork et al., 2020), the operation of peer support through social media (Naslund et al., 2014), and job vacancy postings as an indicator of economic activity (Turrell et al., 2019).

Naturally occurring data can be used in conjunction with elicited data. Researchers can analyse naturally occurring data and use this analysis as the basis of a survey or focus group; Shannon used this methodology in his investigation into the use of Tumblr as a source of peer education within the trans community (Shannon, 2022; Sharp & Shannon, 2020). According to Goldstone and Lupyan (2016) naturally occurring data can also be used to:

- provide external validation for experimental results (do the predictions made based on experimentally generated data hold true in real-world settings?);

- develop experiments to gain insights into real-world outcomes (observing a natural phenomenon and designing experiments to determine what makes it work);

- discover patterns of information that are underlying in real-world environments; and

- inform the construction of computational models of behaviour or cognition.

Big data

The omnipresence of the internet has generated an exponential increase in the amount of data generated by online activities, leading to research on and using what has been termed 'big data'. Kitchin (2013, p. 262) defines big data as:

- huge in *volume*, consisting of terabytes or petabytes of data;

- high in *velocity*, being created in or near real time;

- diverse in *variety* in type, being structured and unstructured in nature, and often temporally and spatially referenced;

- *exhaustive* in scope, striving to capture entire populations or systems (n = all);

- fine-grained in *resolution*, aiming to be as detailed as possible, and uniquely *indexical* in identification;

- *relational* in nature, containing common fields that enable the conjoining of different data sets; and

- *flexible*, holding the traits of extensionality (can add new fields easily) and scalability (can expand in size rapidly).

Subsequent definitions of big data rest on four V's: volume, velocity, variety and either veracity (data integrity and authenticity) or value (the financial or research value of the data to the organization or study) (Stieglitz et al., 2018).

Youtie, Porter and Huang (2017) chart the rise of social science research about big data. Big data offers a myriad of benefits to researchers:

- Big data allows for access to rich, detailed, interrelated, timely and low-cost data that allows for a wider scale, sophisticated and fine-grained insight into the social world (Kitchin, 2013);

- it provides real-time data, as opposed to temporally bound (and expensive) data sets such as census data (Goldstone & Lupyan, 2016); and

- it allows for the collection of granular and characteristics about thousands of individuals at a single point in time and longitudinally (Adjerid & Kelley, 2018).

Small data

Historically academic knowledge has been built on studies based on data that has been produced in highly controlled ways using sampling techniques that limit the scope, temporality, size and number of variables in order to define and limit the levels of error, bias and uncertainty in the research (Adjerid & Kelley, 2018; Goldstone & Lupyan, 2016). With the advent of big data, such research can be defined as 'small data' studies and are characterized by their limited volume, limited number of variables with data generated in response to specific questions (Kitchin & Lauriault, 2015). Kitchin and Lauriault (2015) argue that while small data studies are no longer as prominent in the research landscape, such research remains valuable, as:

- small data studies have a long record of being able to answer specific questions;

- small data studies can be linked and scaled through developing infrastructures, thereby increasing their value through sharing and combining; and

- small data are less vulnerable to issues associated with big data (such as dataveillance, social sorting, control creep and anticipatory governance), where data is used for purposes for which they were never intended.

In the context of online research, small data is differentiated from big by features other than volume. For example, while census data is a very large data set, it is not considered big data as it lacks velocity (it is not created in real-time, but rather it represents one point in time). Small data captures samples rather than entire populations, small data is not typically flexible and scalable, it has low variety, it lacks relationality with other data sets. As Kitchin notes 'small data studies thus seek to mine gold from working a narrow seam, whereas big data studies seek to extract nuggets through open-pit mining, scooping up and sieving huge tracts of land' (2016, p. 35). In the context of online research both data types have value for research; however, small data research is typically less costly as the data is easier to resource, collect, store, sort and analyse. As stated by boyd and Crawford, the 'size of data should fit the research question being asked; in some cases, small is best' (2012, p. 670).

Other ways of understanding online data: Thick, rich, lively

Data can be classified in ways other than volume. Online data can be 'thick' or 'rich' (to use traditional qualitative terms). Data considered to be thick or rich is data that are detailed and complete enough to allow for meaning to be made, such as detailed accounts of the cultural practices being studied, or data that is difficult to quantify such as emotions and stories (Latzko-Toth et al., 2017). For example, a big data set may be able to show how many tweets were made in a given time span, by how many individuals, comprising of how many and which hashtags. While identifying these large-scale patterns may be useful, thick data (such as that generated through interviews with Twitter/X users) can shed light on how people use Twitter/X, why they use it and how they understand their use (Marwick, 2013).

To overcome the issue of dealing with an overwhelming mass of online data Latzko-Toth et al. (2017) suggest reducing the breath of data collection while enhancing the depth or thickness of each data point. They advocate achieving this though a layering approach to online data. When undertaking online research based on a small data set the first step in the layering process is contextualization – when did the online practice emerge, what are the affordances of the technology and what are the surrounding cultural practices? The second layer is description – the production of thick description of the practices being studied. The third layer, signification, captures users experience and the meaning they make from it. This approach to thickening data (contextualization, description, and signification) means that even a small number of cases or datapoints can yield insight and allow for meaning making (Latzko-Toth et al., 2017).

Digital data may also be understood as being 'lively'. Deborah Lupton (2016) characterizes data as being 'lively' in various ways. Lively data is:

1. data about life itself;
2. digital data that is dynamic, being reconfigured through digital interactions and repurposed by different actors and agencies;
3. data that is a part of the global knowledge economy contributing to livelihoods in commercial, managerial, government and research endeavors; and
4. Data that has become an influential part of people's everyday lives, affecting behaviours, beliefs and even life chances via the predictions developed from algorithmic analysis (Lupton, 2016, p. 40).

Lupton's use of the term 'lively' to describe digital data reminds us that data is not static it is connected to living people and changing systems. Regardless of how online data is characterized it is always a constructed artefact that is not value neutral. Understanding the purposes and process behind the generation of the data used for research shapes methodological decision-making about analysis and interpretation (Luka & Millette, 2018).

Publicly available data sets

Much online data can be difficult to access. Small data such as that produced within academia, public institutions, non-government organizations, and private companies can be restricted in access, and much big data are produced by the private sector and are likely to be protected by proprietary licensing (Kitchin, 2016).

One way to access online data is to use publicly accessible data sets (Perry, 2018). Numerous governments are moving to make government administrative data freely available so sites such as http://data.gov (USA), http://open-data.europa.en/en (European Union Open Data Portal) and http://data.gov.uk (UK) provide data that is accessible to social researchers.

Several websites and social media platforms also provide accessible data, for example: Amazon http://aws.amazon.com/datasets, Facebook https://developers.facebook.com/docs/graph-api, and Google www.google/publicdata/directory. Numerous websites, apps and companies that offer an Application Programming Interface (API) also provide access to the data collected through their API, so it is worth exploring what data is available in the beginning stages of a research project.

Gathering and working with online data

When working with online data, researchers must consider how they will access, collect, store and clean their data prior to analysis. In large research projects involving big data, data scientists provide expertise regarding the collection, storage, cleaning and analysis of data. Storage of data is an important consideration as the data needs to be secure as many countries have laws governing where personal data is permitted to be stored due to differing legal frameworks which allow foreign governments access to data from other countries. If cloud storage is being utilized in the research, researchers need to be aware of the data protection offered and where the data is being stored (Charlesworth, 2015).

To collect large data sets computer-assisted methods can be employed such as data-scraping (sometimes called web scraping or web harvesting) – where data from websites is automatically collected from websites and converted into structured data for analysis. APIs can also be used to retrieve online data in a controlled manner, whereas data scrapping typically involves the automated extraction of a large amount of data from websites sometimes without the permission or knowledge of the website owner.

Researchers accessing online data need to consider the inherent bias of the data and the collection methods – using an API with a social media platform does not provide access to all content (as many social media accounts are private, and not all social media platforms allow APIs full access to all content), and in using social media for research the population is limited to those with access to the technology, those whose profiles are not private and people who post more frequently (McFarland et al., 2016; Reynolds & Quinton, 2018). The limitations of the data collection are therefore both technical and social and lead to inherent bias in the data sample.

Data analysis techniques

Depending on the size of the data set, analysing online data can be a complex task. Data analytics refers to processes involved in the examination and interpretation of data to uncover insights, patterns and underlying relationships. This analysis can be descriptive, diagnostic or predictive. Predictive analysis uses statistical models and machine learning algorithms to make predictions about future events.

When undertaking research using naturally occurring or big data the analysis might vary from that of traditional qualitative or quantitative analysis. Such data requires statistical analysis methods suitable for exploring factors which cannot be experimentally manipulated (Goldstone & Lupyan, 2016). Goldstone and Lupyan note that with 'most theoretically motivated questions, there are appropriate and readily available analysis techniques' such as 'correlation, regression, multidimensional scaling, clustering, network analysis, kernel density estimation, Markov models, autoregressive models, detrended fluctuation analysis, Directed Acyclic Graphs, Granger causality, Bayes nets, and machine learning algorithms' (2016, p. 550). There are numerous resources available online to help researchers with the data analysis demands that come with using large data sets (Udacity, Udemy and Khan Academy provide free courses, and many universities offer MOOCs designed to develop researchers' skills. There are also numerous online tools available for analysing data, creating data visualizations and creating predictive models using machine learning algorithms).

While big data is associated with the predictive aims of quantitative methods, the interpretative concerns of qualitative methods are increasingly being employed with online data (Karamshuk et al., 2017; Mockler, 2020a, 2020b). Karamshuk and colleagues (2017) used a machine learning algorithm to automatically code emotive responses on Twitter, allowing for analysis of a volume of tweets that would not otherwise have been possible. From a corpus of nearly 6,000 newspaper articles, Mockler (2020a) was able to trace the shift in discourse regarding national literacy testing in Australia over the period of 2008–18. Bednarek et al. (2021) argue that the technical requirements of using these kinds of computational methods can prevent many social scientists from engaging in this kind of research. However, they argue that it is possible to repurpose computer-assisted linguistic analysis tools to make computationally assisted analysis of large naturally occurring data sets more accessible.

In the analysis of online data, traditional methods of quantitative and qualitative analysis are being supplemented with computational and hybrid methods of analysis (Karamshuk et al., 2017). Lewis and colleagues argue that a blend of computational methods and manual methods of content analysis yield fruitful results, augmenting the rigor and contextual sensitivity of manual coding with the large-scale capacity and algorithmic accuracy of computational methods (Lewis et al., 2013). When using online data, the research process is the same as that employed with data derived from offline sources, however, the volume of data involved and the research purposes may necessitate different types of analysis, some of which could include computational models and machine learning.

In summary

The internet is a vast global network of connected devices. The activity that takes place on this network provides extensive data for researchers – online data offers insight into most aspects of human life and interaction (Reynolds & Quinton, 2018). Most online data is naturally occurring, it has not been generated through the activities of researchers but exists independently of research. While online data can be classified in a variety of ways (big, small, thick, lively, etc.), to be useful to researchers it needs to be collected, stored, cleaned and analysed. There are a variety of online tools to help researchers with this. To make best use of online data, researchers need to consider the research question that they are seeking to answer and design their study accordingly.

Further reading

For further insight into how the internet has changed many aspects of human life see *The SAGE Handbook of Digital Society* (Edwards et al., 2022). Handbooks available to aid researchers in online research include *The Sage Handbook of Online Research Methods* (Fielding et al., 2016), *The SAGE Handbook of Social Media Research Methods* (Quan-Haase & Sloan, 2022) and *Second International Handbook of Internet Research* (Hunsinger et al., 2020). Other useful texts for researchers include *Internet Research Methods* (Hewson et al., 2015), *Big Data and Social Science* (Kreuter et al., 2020) and *Digital Social Research* (Veltri, 2019). Guidance in using publicly available data sets is offered by Perry's (2018) book *Maximising Social Science Research through Publicly Accessible Data Sets*. Texts that provide support for the analysis of online data include *Data Analysis for Social Science* (LLaudet & Kosuke, 2023) and *From Social Science to Data Science* (Hogan, 2022).

CHAPTER THREE

Ethics and online research

The ubiquity of the internet and increased online social interaction presents researchers with new ways to study people. With this abundance of opportunity, it can be easy to focus on the 'how to' of online research, yet it is just as important to consider the 'whether to' and 'what to do' questions of research ethics. Those who are new to the process of institutional ethics approval might want to read this chapter alongside a more general book such as *Research Ethics and Integrity for Social Scientists* (Israel, 2015) or *Research Ethics in the Real World* (Kara, 2018).

Online researchers can bypass gatekeepers, access semi-private information, harvest, reuse and re-analyse data more easily than has previously been possible. Therefore, it is important to ensure that ethical practice remains current where changing technological capacity complicates issues such as confidentiality, privacy and consent. As online research on such phenomena as terrorism and fascism can put researchers at risk, researcher safety has emerged as a contemporary issue in research ethics.

Ethics in online research

Many of the ethical issues which researchers need to address prior to undertaking online research require the adoption of similar ethical practices as those employed in research involving human participants (Barrow et al., 2022); however, given the complexity of the internet guidelines based on solely human subjects are considered inadequate (Conway, 2021; McInroy, 2016; Suomela et al., 2019). The prevailing view, initially advanced by the Association of Internet Researchers (AOIR) (2002), is that online environments present challenges beyond what is encountered in offline research contexts. The ethical decision-making guidelines developed by the AOIR have been updated twice, with each iteration taking account of the increased complexity of available online social and research tools (franzke et al., 2020; Markham et al., 2012).

The generally accepted definition of Internet Research Ethics is:

The analysis of ethical issues and application of research ethics principles as they pertain to research conducted on and in the Internet. Internet-based research, broadly defined, is research which utilizes the Internet to collect information through an online tool, such as an online survey; studies about how people use the Internet, e.g., through collecting data and/or examining activities in or on any online environments; and/or, uses of online datasets, databases, or repositories. (Buchanan & Zimmer, 2021, n.p)

This chapter provides an overview of ethical issues and challenges presented by online research. The complexity of online research necessitates ethical reflection. The varied contexts of online research mean that there is no one ethical approach that fits all situations and populations, so ethical pluralism is advocated (franzke et al., 2020). Given the changing affordances of the internet, 'being "ethical" in online research is a practice that is constantly negotiated, requiring ongoing reflexivity and engagement by the researcher' (Fileborn, 2016, p.102).

Case study: User-generated ideology in the age of Jeremy Corbyn and social media

During the 2015 UK Labour Party Leadership Election Christian Fuchs sought to answer the questions 'How has Jeremy Corbyn during the Labour Leadership Election been framed in an ideological manner in discourses on Twitter and how have such ideological discourses been challenged?' (Fuchs, 2018). The study took place when Corbyn was standing for leadership of the Labour Party in the context of his negative framing in the media (Fuchs, 2016). Fuchs argues that much more research attention has been paid to progressive, left-wing social movements in research into social media for political communication; with comparatively fewer studies that focus on far-right politics, despite the far-right being effective in using social media for political communication (2018). He argues that research needs to be undertaken on the diversity of social movements despite the ethical challenges with respect to privacy, anonymity, informed consent and researcher safety. Fuchs (2016) used ideology critique to analyse tweets collected during the final phases of the Labour Party's 2015 Leadership election. This analysis showed how user-generated ideology framed Jeremy Corbyn in particular ways through discourse on scapegoating, the economy, foreign politics, culture and authoritarianism.

In total, 32,298 tweets mentioning Jeremy Corbyn and a 'smear' word were collected between 22 August and 13 September 2015 (Fuchs, 2016). The smear words were first identified as being keywords in anti-socialist discourses. All tweets collected and analysed included 'Corbyn' plus one of the following: anti-Semite, anti-Semitic, chaos, clown, commy, communism, communist, loony, Marx, Marxist, pinko, red, reds, socialism, socialist, Stalin, Stalinist, terrorist, violent, violence. In exploring the ideologies generated by Twitter users, Fuchs has been able to show that anti-socialism on Twitter is 'an old ideology expressed in new ways. . . . It is a re-contextualisation of ideological discourse' (Fuchs, 2016, p. 393).

Informed consent

In undertaking this research Fuchs needed to consider the ethical implications of exploring and reporting political commentary. Internet research is to be conducted in a manner that ensures users are not harmed by its analyses. Fuchs took a critical-realist approach to ethics in this study (2018). In line with the position of the British Psychological Society who suggest that online observation should only occur where users can reasonably expect observation by strangers, Fuchs considered that online political commentary by Twitter users in the time of an election would be expected to be observed by persons not known to such Twitter users. In this context, Fuchs made the decision that informed consent was not required from those whose tweets were included in the analysis. Given the highly political nature of the analysis, seeking consent from users may in this instance put the researcher at risk.

Issues highlighted

Fuchs' study highlights some of the complexities of the ethics of online research. In offline research, people would usually need to give informed consent for their political opinions to be included in a research study. However, because of the public nature of political tweets it was determined that informed consent was not required in this case. Fuchs gave differential privacy protection to users. The identities of non-public figures were protected, and their tweets anonymized. Public figures were not anonymized as their tweets were intended to reach a wide public audience (Fuchs, 2018). In this case study, users' identities were provided different levels of protection depending upon who they were.

In quoting tweets, even where their usernames were anonymized, there is a possibility that users can be identified (Zook et al., 2017). Some researchers would not report data in this way, they would not use direct quotes that could be sourced to the original poster, perhaps choosing to paraphrase to avoid easy identification (Barnes, 2021; Corple & Linabary, 2020). In thinking through data to be collected, issues of aggregation and individual and group re-identification need to be considered (Locatelli, 2020). In this type of study, the researcher is at risk of harm, potentially from users or from the material they are studying (Conway, 2021). In this case Fuchs used a data scrapping tool to collect the data and did not reveal himself to users.

Privacy

The growth of social media has led to increased self-disclosure across multiple platforms by internet users. Many people provide details of their 'private' lives through tweets, Instagram images, status updates, video and blogs which are publicly available. This blurring of the divide between public and private creates difficulties for researchers who need to consider whether users' perceptions of privacy align with the platform that they are using. As Fileborn notes public accessibility 'does not necessarily mean the data were intended or perceived as public' (2016, p. 103). To negotiate privacy issues, Yadlin-Segal et al. propose the following guiding questions: 'What are the ways in which participants are made aware of the research and researcher, how do they perceive privacy, and how is this privacy maintained?' (2020, p. 176).

Research has found a lack of agreement among internet users regarding what constituted a public space (Mackenzie, 2017). Online researchers have attempted to define public data to be either

1. accessible to anyone with an internet connection; or
2. data or activity that is perceived to public by users (such as those holding public Twitter/X accounts for example).

However, scrolling through public Twitter/X feeds turns up material that is both ephemeral and personal and which the individuals involved may not be comfortable about being reproduced in different contexts. This can sometimes leave researchers in the difficult position of making subjective judgements about what users would want or intend and in which the legal right to access and reproduce material may not fully satisfy moral and ethical concerns about doing so. The situation is more straightforward in spaces which require memberships, permissions and password access. These are enclosed publics which offer users some degree of privacy and where postings wouldn't be considered public data.

In general, the agreed principle is 'the greater the acknowledged publicity of the venue, the less obligation there may be to protect individual privacy' (Ess and Association of Internet Researchers Working Committee, 2002, p. 5). But what is public and private online is rarely a simple binary. As Zook et al. (2017) note, looking at a single posting by a user is ethically different than analysing an individual's entire social media history. Privacy considerations also extend to groups; some groups are vulnerable and historically discriminated against (Zook et al., 2017). In determining whether a particular space is or is not public, issues of informed consent are raised. What right do internet users have to determine whether information that they have disclosed online should be used by researchers?

Informed consent

In 2014 a study about emotional contagion in social networks was published (Kramer et al., 2014) sparking debate about the ethical requirement for informed consent. In the *emotional contagion* study Facebook users had their feeds manipulated such that positive or negative (or neither in the control condition) posts were removed. A small (but statistically significant) effect was found suggesting that emotional states can spread through social networks. The programming code had been deliberately altered to manipulate users' results and intentional deception had occurred as users were not informed that this had taken place. There are three aspects of ethical concern here: 'the absence of user consent to participate in research, the presence of intentional deception, and the complete lack of protection for human subjects' (Benbunan-Fich, 2017, p. 201). This research has the potential to advance understanding about how ideas are spread through social networks. Are such findings worth it if informed consent is bypassed? Researchers working under ethical guidelines and institutional requirements (e.g. those of an institutional review board or human research ethics committee) would not have to option to conduct research like this without convincing their institutional ethics committee that the research was worthwhile and would be ethically conducted.

In general, informed consent is a standard requirement of research involving people; its purpose is to make participants aware of the research and provide them with the option of not being included in the study (Benbunan-Fich, 2017). The amount of information to disclose when seeking consent presents issues for researchers. To provide too much detail may result in participants being 'primed' and altering their usual behaviour, yet consent forms and/or information statements should include a description of the study and an outline of possible benefits and risks so that participants can make an informed decision about participation

(Benbunan-Fich, 2017). In disciplines such as economics or psychology, deception in research is not uncommon; such studies require a good case to justify contravening informed consent. Researchers need to demonstrate that in undertaking their research they are going to minimize harm and debrief participants (Wang & Kitsis, 2013).

Any research where there is risk of harm to participants requires consent. However, some researchers argue that in certain circumstances there are weaker grounds for requiring consent (Elgesem et al., 2015). Elgesem and colleagues maintain that consent is not required when using non-private information that has been posted in a public forum, such as the research undertaken by Fuchs (2016) described above. For research in 'private' online spaces (password provided, members-only spaces) consent should be sought from potential participants. Obtaining consent in situations where covert observation is taking place is not without difficulties . Giaxoglou's (2017) attempts to obtain consent with Facebook users were thwarted, as not being 'friends' with those she sent private messages to, her messages went into spam.

The issue of consent becomes more complicated in studies undertaken with large data sets. In such research it would be impractical, financially burdensome or time-consuming to seek informed consent from all individuals whose data formed part of the study. Fuchs's 2016 study, for example, involved tweets from thousands of people. Some researchers solve this dilemma by seeking consent, after observation has taken place, from users whose data would be quoted in the reporting of the study (Mackenzie, 2017). This means that consent is sought after the research has been undertaken. Researchers studying in online communities have experienced backlash from moderators and commentators on online community boards (Sugiura, Wiles & Pope, 2017). Some review boards are prepared to waive the requirement for consent in cases where there is minimal risk of harm to users and where the research could not practically be undertaken without such a waiver (Sugiura et al., 2017). Chua describes their decision not to seek informed consent as contributing the smooth execution of their research; however, this decision was not taken lightly and involved ensuring that their actions were in line with the terms and conditions of the online space that they were studying (2022).

Anonymity

Anonymity refers to a situation where no one, including researchers, can link a participants' identity to any information that forms part of the research project. Confidentiality describes the situation where researchers know participants' identity but have taken steps to prevent this from being revealed to others. While anonymity and confidentiality are frequent features of offline research, the nature of the internet might mean that a researcher cannot easily guarantee participants this level of protection. Even in situations where researchers do not know the sources of their data, it may be possible through the way that it is harvested, stored or reported, for others to link data to its source and identify people (Zimmer, 2018; Zook et al., 2017). Researchers can mitigate against this through taking active steps, such as paraphrasing or changing data to make it harder to trace via search engine. Although it may be difficult to ensure complete anonymity, researchers should employ protective measures such as removing all identifying features (names, locations, URLs, etc.) prior to publication (Sugiura et al., 2017). Presentation of data in research reporting needs to be thought through as verbatim quotes can be traced back to their original source (Corple & Linabary, 2020). Qualitative data can be presented through reporting of themes, for example, without directly quoting participants (Barnes, 2021).

In cases such as public blogs, not attributing the source may violate the author's copyright. In addition to issues of copyright, some participants may want to be acknowledged while others would prefer to have their words reported anonymously. It is not always necessary nor appropriate to maintain anonymity for users. In Fuchs's (2016) study, anonymity was given to non-public figures but not to public figures, institutions and bots. Chua (2022) employed 'attribution with anonymisation' in their study of an online discussion forum. A specific online discussion forum was acknowledged as the source of the data, but all user quotes were anonymized in the publication of the study. This was possible because the discussion forum was not accessible to public so the source of research could be acknowledged while protecting the identities of those quoted in the study. In considering anonymity and confidentiality, the accessibility and public availability of the data source, the attribution required, the storage and protection of data, need to be considered and decided upon depending upon the context and purpose of the research, the sources of data and the privacy laws governing the research.

Legal issues

It is not sufficient to be ethical in research; legal requirements, such as the General Data Privacy Regulation (the EU data privacy regulations) (Ess, 2020) or the US Common Rule (franzke et al., 2020), have implications for the conduct of online research. The storage of research data collected needs to be carefully considered. Many countries have laws governing where data is permitted to be stored due to differing legal frameworks which allow foreign governments access to data from other countries. If cloud storage is being utilized in the research, researchers need to be aware of the data protection offered and where the data is being stored (Charlesworth, 2015). Researchers also need to be aware of copyright law and attribution requirements when studying user-generated content (UGC). While the copyright and fair use laws vary by country, care must be taken to follow law in the jurisdiction where the research material is being published (Pihlaja, 2017).

Online platforms, such as Twitter/X, have terms and conditions that apply to users, as well as those (such as researchers) who seek to use data from the platform. Researchers need to ensure that they are not in breach of these while considering the potential experience of users and their expectations for privacy (Chua, 2022). What is legal and permissible according to the terms and conditions in each context may not always be ethical, so researchers need to meet the legal, regulatory and their own institutional requirements as a minimum. In determining ethical conduct contextual ethical frameworks provide guidance. However, the ethical principles underpinning these vary. Ess (2020) notes that the initial AIOR research guidelines (2002) have a utilitarian basis (the greatest good for the greater number) and a focus on individual rights. This contrasts with the Norwegian Research Ethics Committee's guidelines for internet research which has a stronger emphasis on human dignity and human relations (Ess, 2020). The AIOR

Internet Research: Ethical Guidelines 3.0 (franzke et al., 2020) are based on the concept of ethical pluralism and provide guidance for negotiating national and international laws, as well as a variety of ethics norms such as feminist, ethics of care, utilitarian and deontological.

Participant vulnerability

When research involves vulnerable groups, such as children (Graham et al., 2013; Third et al., 2015) they should be afforded extra protection from the potential of harm. Online research is complicated as it is not always easy to determine whether users in a specific context are children or not. In their research into teen readers Dezuanni et al. (2022) sought Instagram and TikTok creators who were 'identifiably' over the age of eighteen. Where data is collected from contexts in which it is not possible to determine whether it has come from children, the data should be treated as though the sources are vulnerable.

While children are clearly a vulnerable group, other internet users are vulnerable for reasons not necessarily related to their age. Research into mental health or LGBTQI cultures involves potentially vulnerable internet users (Crawford et al., 2019; McInroy, 2016), and researchers should have a means of supporting participants should their research cause distress. Zook et al. (2017) urge caution in big data research as searches of large data sets for population-wide effects can stigmatize individuals or groups or be reused for invasive research. They note that some communities have historically experienced discriminatory data-driven policies, so seemingly innocuous public data sets need to be used cautiously – 'start with the assumption that data are people (until proven otherwise) and use it to guide your analysis' (Zook et al., 2017, p. 2).

Researcher safety

One of the abiding principles of research ethics is that no harm should come to those involved. This includes the researcher. Some types of online research, such as digital ethnography can involve risk of harm to the researcher, as Fuchs (2018) makes clear in his chapter titled 'Dear Mr. Neo-Nazi, can you please give me your informed consent so that I can quote your Fascist tweet?'. There are various options for presence and disclosure available to online users, from the use of one's real name, or pseudonyms, to anonymous 'lurking'. Researchers can fully disclose themselves and their purposes in research (Mackenzie, 2017). In other cases, 'research subjects generally remain fully in the dark that any research is taking place and, in fact, are often led to believe that the researcher is a fellow traveller of whatever variety (e.g. a right-wing extremist, jihadi,drug dealer, etc.)' (Conway, 2021, p. 372).

When working in online spaces, researchers need to consider 'when is the appropriate time for disclosure or undercover research?' (Yadlin-Segal, Tsuria and Bellar, 2020, p. 176). There is considerable ethical debate about the appropriateness of researcher concealment; however, for reasons of safety this is considered permissible in fields such as terrorism research. As online controversies such as Gamergate (an online controversy in 2014 and 2015 over ethics in journalism, misogyny, feminism, diversity and progressivism in video game culture, that included harassment campaigns against women using the hashtag #Gamergate) have shown, discussion of particular topics in specific online spaces carry a risk of doxxing or harassment (Aghazadeh et al., 2018) for those who are perceived to be outsiders. An evaluation of the safety of the online space is required to balance the requirement of disclosure and researcher safety.

Suomela et al. note that psychological safety is also a concern (2019). They describe the potential for harm to members of their research team who were viewing misogynistic content and hate speech while collecting data from the internet forum 4chan. To moderate this risk, they deleted what they termed 'toxic data' and halted its collection. There are times when such risk is not foreseeable in the design phase of the study. Ethical conduct involves constant evaluation and reflexivity, and the research process should be amended to protect those involved where it becomes apparent that harm is occurring. Self-care for the researchers may be required to mitigate the risk of undertaking sensitive research; Schulz et al. (2022) provide guidance on how such care can be undertaken.

In summary

Online research should be conducted in a manner where issues of privacy, informed consent, anonymity and confidentiality, legal issues and terms and conditions, participant vulnerability and researcher safety are considered. When researchers make ethical choices, weighing up competing concerns and negotiating multiple factors, it is important to be transparent in the explanation of the decisions made (Suomela et al., 2019). While there are no standard approaches, ethical consideration for participants and data sources, institutional review board guidelines and jurisdiction requirements should all form part of the decision-making process. The onus is on the researcher to manage risk and avoid harm to the individuals and groups in their study, but applying traditional research guidelines to online research does not work well due to the complexity and changing nature of online environments (Sugiura et al., 2017). A process – and context-oriented approach suggests ethics-as-method; that is, 'our choice of methods vis-à-vis given research questions and design evoke specific ethical issues – but these in turn (should) shape our methodological choices' (franzke et al., 2020, p. 4). Ethical decision-making does not just occur at the beginning of a study but should take place at every stage of the research process.

Further reading

A deeper examination of the issues described here is provided by *Internet research ethics* (Elgesem et al., 2015); *Digital ethics: Media, communication and society* (Fuchs, 2022); *The datafied society: Studying culture through data* (Schäfer & Es, 2017); and *Internet research ethics for the social age* (Zimmer & Kinder-Kurlanda, 2017). A focused discussion of the ethical implications of the use of deception in research is provided by Marzano (2021) and Ortmann (2019).

The work done by the AOIR is useful for understanding the iterative development of ethical decision-making resources for online research (Ess & Association of Internet Researchers Working Committee, 2002; franzke et al., 2020; Markham, Buchanan & Association of Internet Researchers Working Committee, 2012).

CHAPTER FOUR

Online surveys

Online questionnaires have become abundant. They offer value to researchers in terms of cost, speed of data collection and analysis and access to respondents; as a result they are used for a wide variety of purposes.

Academic survey research makes up a small sub-set of the surveys that any individual might encounter and a tiny sub-set of all the things that are vying for attention on the internet. As a result, many people may consider online surveys as little better than spam. For this reason, academic researchers must think carefully about the pitfalls of online surveys and remain aware that engaging a target population in an online survey may not be straightforward.

This chapter explores some of the issues surrounding online surveys, provides readers with an overview of the method, and a range of practical advice on how to develop effective surveys, maximize response rates and enhance data quality.

Case study: Surveying athletes about their careers

Giancarlo Condello and colleagues (Condello et al., 2019) were interested in how athletes combine participation in elite sport with higher education and pursuing a 'dual' career alongside sport. They decided to survey participants in the Universiade, an international multi-sport event for university athletes.

They developed a thirty-one-question survey exploring a variety of issues identified through a literature review as being likely to influence the careers of athletes. It covered demographics, engagement in sport and in university, familiarity with dual career policies and support. The survey was mainly designed with pre-coded questions, but also included some open-text questions.

The researchers negotiated access to all Universiade participants and distributed the survey via country representatives. This was followed by three chasing messages over the next fifteen days. The survey received 426 responses (approximately 6 per cent of the athletes participating in the competition). The sample over-represented participants from Europe and Oceania and under-represented those from Asia, America and Africa.

The data were coded and analysed statistically in SPSS: key findings included the fact that most respondents experience substantial challenges in combining sport, study and career, that few were aware of dual career policies and that most reported receiving some support to help them with managing their dual career. There were significant variations between student-athletes from different countries.

Condello et al. note that the response rate to their survey was low. They reflected that this may have been because (1) the survey was sent at the end of the event when most of the student-athletes were on vacation; (2) because some student-athletes came from countries where sport and education are combined and might have considered the dual career issue as irrelevant; and (3) due to language issues as the survey was conducted in English. These issues of recruitment timing, interest, relevance, culture and language are key for all surveys.

Issues highlighted

Issues of sampling and response rates remain as some of the most challenging issues in online surveys. Interpreting nonresponse can be as critical to the analysis as analysing the responses received.

Low participation rates in online surveys are common, but because it is viable to access a large population at low cost, this can still result in substantial numbers of responses. Researchers are then faced with challenges about how to interpret the data they have collected and consider whether it is possible to say that it is in any way representative of the larger population. One of the key issues that affects this is how access has been negotiated, as this shapes understanding of what the population actually is. In this case the researchers were able to identify a finite population and have a reasonable expectation that they had been able to access everyone in this population. This is often not the case in online surveys.

Online surveys open up the possibility for cross-national and cross-cultural studies, but this raises questions as to how the survey will be interpreted in different contexts.

Using online surveys

This chapter focuses on using survey methodologies online, but most of the basic principles of surveys remain the same as with onsite methods. Rather than discuss these basics, the chapter focuses on how these issues are recontextualized by moving a survey online.

Those new to surveying might want to read this chapter alongside a more general book such as *Survey Research and Sampling* (Eichhorn, 2022), *Internet, Phone, Mail* and *Mixed–Mode Surveys* (Dillman et al., 2014) or *The Practice of Survey Research* (Rule et al., 2016). Any of these books (alongside many others) will provide the reader with a solid introduction to surveys.

When to use an online survey?

Deciding on what methodology(ies) to use to address a particular set of research questions is one of the most critical decisions for a researcher. If a survey-based methodology is chosen the researcher has a range of decisions about the most appropriate way to collect data, engage participants and manage the survey. As surveys can be conducted face-to-face, by post, by telephone and by a range of other mechanisms, the decision to use an online survey must be weighed up against the alternatives.

Since the first edition of this book the use of online surveys has become increasingly pervasive. In many cases online surveys will be the default option for researchers investigating a range of phenomenon. The growing importance of the internet as a medium for survey research has been driven by three major socio-technological trends: growing broadband connectivity and an associated increase in the usage of the internet; smart mobile device ownership; and social media (Evans & Mathur, 2018). Yet it remains important not to fall into the assumption that an online survey is the best approach for all studies.

Drawing together recent research on online surveys, we can identify the following advantages on using online surveys (Ball, 2019; Chang & Vowles, 2013; Evans & Mathur, 2018):

- **Access** to a wide range of (potentially global) populations.

- **Control over survey design** including the ability to offer interactive, multimedia and personalized question types, automated reminders and follow-up messages.

- **Ease of response for participants,** allowing them to access surveys from where they are and answer at their own pace.

- **Privacy for respondents** including the minimization of interviewer influence and bias. This can be particularly important when dealing with sensitive subjects.

- **Speed, convenience and cost-effectiveness** for the researcher.

Online surveys are not appropriate in all circumstances and with all populations. Furthermore, there are several downsides associated with them. We can summarize these disadvantages as follows:

- **Impersonal** data collection can make it more difficult to clarify when respondents do not understand. This can lead to increased dropout rates.

- **Low response rates,** driven in part by the ubiquity of online surveys.

- **Privacy issues** related to growing public concern about the collection and use of online data.

- **Reliance on technology** to deliver the survey which inevitably raises challenges for those with older and less standard ways of accessing the internet.

- **Sampling issues** as not everyone is equally connected to the internet.

- **Unreliability** with concerns about some participants providing false information.

In many cases the advantages and disadvantages of online surveys are the flip sides of each other.

Sampling. Who is being surveyed?

Researchers need to identify the population that they are researching and consider how the people who are going to complete the survey (the sample) relate to that population. Careful consideration of this issue is important as there are widely articulated concerns about the representativeness of online surveys (Andrade, 2020; Lehdonvirta et al., 2021). Cornesse and Bosnjak (2018) have found that in general online surveys are less representative than face-to-face or postal surveys, but it is important to remember that the mode of delivery is just one among many factors governing representativeness and that not all surveys are seeking statistical representativeness.

There are a range of different approaches that can be used to build a sample. These methodological approaches interact with the tools and technologies that are used to deliver online surveys in a variety of ways. It is beyond the scope of this chapter to discuss the wider literature on sampling (see Blair & Blair, 2014), but the sources of statistical error are the same online as in other forms of survey research. This includes issues related to coverage, sampling, non-response and measurement (Bosnjak et al., 2016).

Online surveys can be used effectively for both probability and nonprobability-based sampling (Fricker, 2016), but to achieve this it is important to think through the population and to consider the approaches that are being used to sample it. This includes the building of a sample frame, consideration of mode effects and what can be done to mitigate them and recognizing the limitations of the sample.

The following questions inspired by Evans and Mathur (2018) can be used to develop a sample:

- How well is the population that you want to research defined and understood? In particularly how well is its use of the internet understood?

- Are you aiming for a sample that is representative of your population and how will an online approach impact on that?

- How respondents will be accessed?

- Will you use a random or non-random sampling approach?

- Will you ask participants to opt in or opt out of your research?

- Can anyone access the survey from outside of the population?

- How many people do you hope or expect to complete your survey?

- How will you monitor who is and is not responding?

- Will you use any incentives to increase response rates?

- Is anyone left out, for example because they are not online?

Designing online questionnaires

Designing an online questionnaire requires researchers to attend to both accessibility (can everyone access the survey) and usability (is the experience of completing the survey a positive one).

Poor accessibility may exclude groups from a survey, for example visually impaired respondents may be unable to complete the survey if it cannot be read by a screen reader or people using older computers may find it difficult if the survey is not backwards compatible. Poor usability will result in your survey being a challenge for everyone. Long, badly worded questions, complex routing and navigation and frequent variations in the question type may leave participants frustrated and result in an increase in dropout rates.

Thankfully a lot of the responsibility for ensuring good accessibility and usability can be addressed by carefully selecting the online survey tool. When making selections look for information about the accessibility of the tool and ask how it deals with different user groups. Most survey tools should be Web Content Accessibility Guidelines (WCAG) compliant (W3C, 2022) as this is an international technical standard for accessibility.

When researchers choose a tool, and design a survey, they should test it and attend to its usability. Is it easy to use or frustrating? Questionnaire should be piloted, ideally using test participants who are drawn from the survey population. Asking these pilot participants questions about how they understand what they are being asked (sometimes called 'cognitive testing') is very instructive for researchers seeking to understand the usability of their questionnaire (Willis, 2017). In addition, Krug (2013) emphasizes the importance of paying attention to existing conventions (what does everyone else's online surveys look like?).

There are several areas to pay attention to in the design of online surveys:

- **Brevity:** Shorter online questionnaires receive higher response rates and experience less dropout than longer ones (Liu & Wronski, 2018; Saleh & Bista, 2017). Given this, there are strong reasons to try and ensure that questionnaires are kept short, and that use is made of routing questions so that respondents are only answering relevant questions.

- **Consistency:** Online questionnaires should be designed to be internally consistent. Respondents are likely to find changes in font, colour and navigation disorientating. Each question type that is introduced (such as multiple choice, multiple answer, ranking and so on) presents respondents with a new usability challenge. In general, choose simple question types which users can parse in a single glance and avoid the proliferation of question types.

- **Functionality:** Survey tools offer a wider range of question types and other functionality such as the opportunity to embed multimedia content into questions. In general, it is best to keep it simple and to only use functionality that is essential for your research questions. Some functionality appears appealing but ultimately has a negative impact on response rates or data quality. For example, Funke (2016) found that slider scales reduce the quantity and quality of data collected (especially on mobile devices).

- **Respondent autonomy:** It is important that the experience of participating in a survey is a positive one. Furthermore, researchers have a duty to conduct research in an ethical way without compulsion. In practice this means that respondents should have the opportunity to decide which questions they answer, when they can exit the questionnaire and whether their data is used or not. Respondents' desire for autonomy is likely to increase where sensitive subjects are researched.

- **Transparency:** Respondents should be able to easily ascertain the purpose, rationale and context of any survey they participate in. In practice this means that background information such as who is undertaking the survey, who is funding it, what the main research questions are, how data will be stored and where findings will be reported should all be available to respondents. A short welcome screen providing a summary of the project, with an associated box to indicate consent, is also a key element of this.

There are many different tools that deliver online surveys. It is not possible to provide a list of such tools because the market is shifting quickly, but judicious use of a search engine will generate numerous options for you to investigate. It can also be useful to look for review sites to help in your decision-making.

In choosing a survey tool it may be useful to consider some of the following issues:

- **Accessibility and usability:** These issues have already been discussed above, but it is important that they are attended to at the point at which a tool is being selected.

- **Analysis tools:** Does the tool offer any analysis functionality? This may not be necessary if you are likely to move the data into another format for analysis, but such functionality can be useful to gain a quick overview of progress while the survey is ongoing.

- **Configurability**: How much control is it possible to exert over the way that a particular tool looks/operates. This may relate to basic issues such as colour and font but is also likely to be critical when looking at issues such as page design and routing of questions.

- **Cost**: How much does the tool cost and how is this cost organized, for example, as a monthly subscription, by the number of responses that you receive or per survey?

- **Data security**: You have ethical, and possibly legal, responsibilities to ensure that your data is kept in a secure fashion. Examining the data security of any tool and how far it complies with any relevant legislation is therefore crucial.

- **Ease of use/support**: There are big advantages to choosing a tool that you can easily use yourself without the requirement for technical support.

- **Export formats**: Does the tool allow you to export data into the format in which you will analyse it – for example, SPSS or Excel?

- **Question type**: What range of questions do different tools offer, and do these question types match with your needs?

- **Vendor limits**: Some vendors place limits on things such as the maximum number of questions or the number of respondents. Often these limits can be removed by paying for an advanced licence. Researchers should investigate these limits and match them to their needs.

- **Verification tools**: Does the tool offer any way to verify identity or manage spam? There are a variety of approaches, including the issuing of passwords or the verification against email addresses or other online accounts such as Google or Facebook.

Once a tool has been chosen it is recommended you pilot it to ensure that it is able to deliver the required functionality.

Considering mode

When online surveys were first developing, there was a lot of interest in whether online, face-to-face or postal surveys elicited different kinds of responses and different quality of data. However, more recent research typically estimates the impact of mode on data quality as small or non-existent (Ansolabehere & Schaffner, 2014; Bytzek & Bieber, 2016; Ravert et al., 2015); although as already discussed it can make a difference to the representativeness of the sample. This opens the possibility of using hybrid surveys combining different modes to increase coverage and representativeness (Cornesse & Bosnjak, 2018).

A key new area of thinking about the importance of mode relates to mobile technologies. There has been a massive increase in mobile ownership and in the use of this technology for online surveys (Revilla et al., 2015; Wells, 2015). Even where surveys are not designed for mobile devices they are commonly accessed in this way by some participants (Toepoel & Lugtig, 2015; Wells, 2015).

Surveys need to be adapted for smart phones and other mobile devices (Wells, 2015). Such adaption includes arranging survey buttons vertically and shortening the length of surveys (Stapleton, 2013) as well as using purpose-built survey tools optimized for mobile use. But the adaption of surveys for mobile devices also opens new possibilities for survey research. For example, it is possible to ask participants to take photos of things, to install and test new applications (Revilla et al., 2015) or to use functionality like barcode scanning (Wells, 2015).

There are also range of disadvantages to using mobile devices for surveys including low response rates and the diversity of mobile devices and their functional limitations such as small screen size (Revilla et al., 2015). Respondents using mobile devices are also likely to have a lower commitment to the survey (De Bruijne & Wijnant, 2013) and be more likely to abandon it midway (Wells, 2015). This may be because surveys take longer on mobile devices and because mobile users are more likely to be in locations where they will be disturbed by third parties and strangers (Toninelli & Revilla, 2016; Wells, 2015).

Comparative research between desktops, laptops and mobile devices has found varied effects, with some finding little or no mode effects (Wells et al., 2014; Wells, 2015), while others have found that data gathered through mobile devices is subject to more errors (Struminskaya et al., 2015). Antoun et al. (2017) argue that differences in data quality can largely be accounted for by difficulties in using some survey functionality on mobile devices, suggesting that with better-designed and mobile-optimized surveys these discrepancies would disappear. Respondents working on laptop or desktop machines also may provide longer answers to open-ended questions (Wells, 2015).

Successful recruitment

One of the principal challenges of survey research is convincing participants to complete a questionnaire. Many researchers have discussed whether the growth in online surveys has had a negative impact on response rates. The issue of response rates compared with traditional paper surveys was being discussed as early as 1994 (Schuldt & Totten, 1994). In 1996, Comley used a multi-mode approach and compared the response rates to email and postal surveys. Because of the novelty of the email approach, he achieved a 45 per cent response rate for email and 16 per cent for the same postal survey. However, as the use of online surveys has increased, the response rate has declined with recent meta-analysis finding that web surveys receive lower response rates (by 12 percentage points) than other types of survey (Daikeler et al., 2020). Other research has also noted a marked decline in the response rates to mail surveys, suggesting that issues with mode are not the only thing impacting response rates (Stedman et al., 2019).

Various researchers have tried to estimate the typical response rate associated with online surveys. Van Moi (2017) estimates average response rates are between 6 and 20 per cent, but the response rate will vary by such a myriad of factors that it is unclear as to whether it is useful to suggest a 'typical' response rate.

Researchers have an opportunity to improve recruitment through a range of strategies. Drawing together the literature on improving recruitment provides a range of ideas that can guide researchers (Keusch, 2015; Petrovčič et al., 2016; Saleh & Bista, 2017; Van Mol, 2017):

- **Pre-notify participants** that you intend to survey them.

- Ask a **trusted intermediary** (organization or individual) to introduce the survey to respondents.

- **Personalize the invitation**, highlight that the participant has been *selected*, and set out how it aligns with their interests. Include an explicit plea for help as part of the invitation.

- **Keep the survey as short as possible** and be explicit about the time that it will take.

- **Be clear about how the data will be handled** and the level of confidentiality and anonymity.

- **Provide an incentive** for participants. The most effective incentives are offered up front (LaRose & Tsai, 2014). There is also evidence to support sweepstake style incentives (LaRose & Tsai, 2014), but little to support altruistic incentives such as donating to a charity for respondents (Pedersen & Nielsen, 2016).

- **Use or construct a panel.** It is possible to use a formally constituted online panel to recruit participants. Well-organized panels are designed to offer access to a range of sub-populations and can offer some reassurance about representativeness (Evans & Mathur, 2018). An alternative is for researchers to use gig economy and crowdsourcing tools to access a sample for example, MTurk. This approach raises a range of sampling issues but can be useful for gathering large-scale samples (Heen et al., 2014).

- **Send up to three reminders.** Reminders will increase the number of responses although they may not broaden the diversity of the sample.

Improving data quality

Some research suggests that there are some differences between face-to-face and online surveys in terms of data quality and the patterns of responses. But, as discussed above, mode effect is limited and so it is important to focus on actively improving data quality (Chang & Vowles, 2013; Liu & Wronski, 2018; Ward & Meade, 2018).

A key element of this is thinking about the representativeness of samples. This was raised in the early days of online research with Coomber noting that respondents to online surveys were disproportionately white, male, first world, affluent and educated (Coomber, 1997). However, as the demographics of internet use have broadened this bias is unlikely to hold true. However, this does not mean that an internet sample can be understood to be representative locally, nationally or globally. The ability to achieve any kind of representativeness is highly dependent on researchers' recruitment strategies and likely to be influenced by geography, social-economic position and language among many other factors.

Evidence-based approaches to the enhancement of data quality include the following:

- **Specify the target population carefully** and manage recruitment to ensure that only this population is surveyed.

- **Explicitly encourage participants to be careful in their responses.** Most respondents will want to provide high-quality and consistent data.

- **Screen participants** using logins, IP address verification and screening questions.

- **Reduce survey complexity** by using shorter surveys and simple question formats.

- **Maintain data consistency** by using pairs of key questions to check consistency.

- **Clean data** using IP addresses to remove multiple repetitive responses as well as other forms of data cleaning, for example identifying partial responses, same-across-the-board responses, responses with meaningless data in them and so on.

In summary

Online surveys offer researchers a powerful tool with many advantages. As the online population has grown, such surveys have increasingly become the default approach. However, the use of online surveys is not without challenges in areas such as identity verification, sampling and representativeness. For those working in the quantitative tradition, these issues may pose considerable concerns. Thankfully there is a lively and ever-growing research literature which is examining these issues and developing strategies to address them. In general, as with other online research methods, online surveys should not be viewed as a panacea. Rather, online surveys need to be used carefully and critically and combined with onsite and postal approaches where appropriate.

Further reading

There has been a considerable amount of energy devoted to the discussion and exposition of online survey-based methods. Useful overviews of the area include *Web Survey Methodology* (Callegaro et al., 2014), *The Handbook of Web Surveys* (Biffignandi & Bethlehem, 2021) or *Doing Surveys Online* (Toepoel, 2016). Most general books addressing survey methodology will now address online surveys in a substantial way.

CHAPTER FIVE

Online interviews and focus groups

While the take up of qualitative methods in online research initially lagged behind that of quantitative methods such as online surveys, developments such as improved availability of affordable quality video conferencing software has led to the increased use of qualitative research methods, such as interviews and focus groups, for online research. This chapter explores these online qualitative techniques and provides guidance for their use and considers the relative merits of synchronous, asynchronous, text-based and multimedia interviews.

Those new to qualitative research methods may like to read this chapter along with an introductory text such as Hennink et al.'s (2020) text *Qualitative Research Methods* or *The SAGE Handbook of Interview Research* (Gubrium et al., 2021). For information specifically on interviews see Fujii (2018), *Interviewing in Social Science Research*; Brinkmann and Steinar (2014), *InterViews: Learning the Craft of Qualitative Research Interviewing*; or King et al. (2018) *Interviews in Qualitative Research*. Guidance in the use of focus groups is provided by Krueger and Casey's book (2015) *Focus Groups* or Acocella and Cataldi's text (2021), *Using Focus Groups: Theory, Methodology, Practice*.

Case study: Instagram interviews at cultural sites

Online and onsite worlds interact at cultural sites – having travelled (perhaps far) to see them, tourists can be observed looking at their phones in the presence of cultural artefacts and memorials, yet engagement with these sites can continue through social media after the visit (Hugentobler, 2022). People often use their phones to photograph artefacts, post pictures of their visit and find out more information about the site.

To investigate how tourists engage with cultural sites and memorials using their internet-connected devices, Larissa Hugentobler (2022) employed what she termed an 'Instagram interview'. To recruit participants, Hugentobler created a professional Instagram profile identifying herself as a researcher and linking to her website and institutional profile. She populated her account with her own travel pictures and later added images of herself undertaking fieldwork. Her research focused on how people interacted with the Martin Luther King (MLK) Jr Memorial in Washington, DC.

She searched for photos tagged at the MLK memorial belonging to people with public Instagram accounts. Hugentobler would follow the accounts of those who posted tagged location photos of the memorial and send them direct messages (DMs) inviting them to participate in her research. Participation involved answering questions about their experience of the memorial via Instagram DM. Hugentobler did not follow a prescribed interview schedule but asked participants different questions depending upon their interactions with her. Each question was crafted in response to participants' previous answers. She kept her initial invitation relatively brief – ensuring that the message was short enough to appear on a mobile phone screen without the need for scrolling. For subsequent questions she was guided by how the conversation flowed.

Hugentobler sought to ensure that interview was as natural possible, allowing people to respond via Instagram voice or text message as preferred. Messages and questions were phrased informally and might include emojis in keeping with the communication norms of Instagram. The open-ended questions focused on participants' posts about, and experiences of, the MLK memorial. She found responses were natural and included colloquialisms and typos. Hugentobler received answers to her questions that were deeply personal and thoughtful, reflecting the combination of intimacy and anonymity that can characterize social media platforms such as Instagram.

Issues highlighted

Hugentobler's study demonstrates the increasing entanglement of online and onsite spaces. To understand the meaning to people of their visit to a cultural space, Hugentobler used social media to both recruit and interview participants. She contacted 118 Instagram users and interviewed 22 participants for a response rate of 19 per cent. This self-selection by participants can introduce selection bias as those choosing to partake in the interview are more likely to be interested in the topic than the average person.

The structure of the asynchronous 'Instagram interview' was shaped by the affordances of the app and the norms for interaction and communication in that space. This method demonstrates that online research methods can be used to study offline or onsite behaviour. The asynchronous nature of the interview meant Hugentobler could reach a dispersed population and participants provided longer responses in their own time (this meant that data was being collected over several weeks with each participant). As the research focused on a popular tourist site visited by people from a variety of places, it was beneficial to employ a research method where participation wasn't temporally or geographically bound. The alignment of her tourism research focus and the location-based affordances of Instagram allowed for the targeted collection of data by participants from a variety of places.

Using online qualitative research methods

This chapter focuses on the use of qualitative methods for online research. Qualitative methods are very useful when the research is seeking exploratory rather than explanatory data. Qualitative research has seen a substantial increase in prevalence in the last two decades (Thelwall & Nevill, 2021). While the principles of such methods do not differ significantly between online and onsite application it is worth considering what changes are required when these methods are used online. Rather than rehearse the basics of these methods, this chapter focuses on the decisions that need to be made for the online context.

Interviews have been used in research since the early twentieth century (Platt, 2014). Initial forms of interview which relied on notetaking and the memory of the researcher have been supplanted by technological developments allowing for a variety of interview modes involving text, audio and/or video recording. With online technologies interviews need not occur in-person but can take place through online video, online chat, online email/message board (Namey et al., 2020) or take place in virtual worlds (Salmons, 2015). These options mean that the interviews can involve synchronous or asynchronous communication.

While there are methodological differences between online interviews and focus groups, most of these differences are like those faced by researchers conducting onsite research. In this chapter, interviews, groups interviews and focus groups are treated together in terms of the considerations that need to be attended to when these methods are conducted online. Before proceeding to a discussion of the application of qualitative methods to the online environment it is worth starting with some basic definitions:

- **Interviews** involve an interaction between a researcher and a research participant for the purpose of gathering qualitative data. Interviews typically gather factual and interpretative data and can be underpinned by a variety of approaches (structured/semi-structured/unstructured, life history, narrative, thematic, etc.).

- **Group interviews** use a similar approach to individual interviews but apply this to a group. The group would usually comprise of people with a shared characteristic or context. Group interviews can be especially useful with children, who can feel more comfortable with a group of other children rather than meeting with just the researcher

(Adler et al., 2019). In the group interview data is derived from the group's answers to the questions and their interactions with one another.

- **Focus groups** are a specialized form of group interview in which participants are asked to interact around a specific theme, topic or set of issues (Thelwall & Nevill, 2021). Participants are often selected to be representative of a particular population. Focus groups typically seek to reveal opinions, attitudes, beliefs rather than to establish facts.

Online interviews

Since the first edition of this book the use of online interviews has become more routine. In cases where cost or geographic distance is an issue (Thunberg & Arnell, 2022) or where sensitive issues are being discussed (Adler et al., 2019; Woodyatt et al., 2016) online interviews are an appealing option.

In their comparison of video conference interviews and face-to-face interviews Krouwel et al. (2019) conclude that in-person interviews were 'marginally' superior as the interviewees said a little more. They suggest that the difference is sufficiently modest that time and budget constraints justify the use of online interviews. However, the affective atmosphere of an interview changes when it is conducted online (Adams-Hutcheson & Longhurst, 2017). Some research participants prefer video interviews as they can participate in a setting of their choice (such as the safety of their own home), do not have to meet a stranger in person (Adams-Hutcheson & Longhurst, 2017; Thunberg & Arnell, 2022), and can remain anonymous (Adler et al., 2019). Stewart and Shamdasani argue that the differences between face-to-face and online interviews are being eroded as the developments in technology allow for the creation of social presence online (Stewart & Shamdasani, 2017).

Technical issues are less prevalent (although they remain) than they used to be due to the ubiquity of internet-connected devices and the improved availability of high-quality video conferencing software although not all universities provide researchers with access to the necessary software.

The use of online interviews provides options for alternatives when face-to-face interviews are not possible (Saarijärvi & Bratt, 2021) and offers numerous benefits to researchers (de Villiers et al., 2021; Gray et al., 2020; Shelton & Jones, 2022; Sipes et al., 2022):

- Many participants find it convenient and report ease of use.

- Video offers enhanced personal interface for the discussion of personal topics (such as parenting), alternatively voice-only options can be used for the discussion of sensitive topics (such as sexual identity).

- Ease of incorporation of readily available and accessible technologies (phone, tablet and laptop).

- No travel requirements for researchers or participants.

- Accommodation of participants' needs and preferences.

- Equitable access to media used in the interactions.

- Offers multiple modes of participation.

- In the case of group interview, it can be logistically easier to pull together a group online than to organize an in-person meetup.

Online interviews are not always an appropriate method, depending upon the research focus, contextual circumstances and the target population. Challenges associated with online interviews (Jones et al., 2023; Shelton & Jones, 2022) include:

- the reliance on facilitators' technological knowledge and skills;

- participants' and facilitators' varying familiarity (or lack thereof) with online platforms;

- difficulties of access to, and variable dependability of, online technologies and the internet connection;

- challenges in recruiting and accessing specific populations online, especially those which are defined by geographic location, who it may be easier to interview face to face;

- the challenges of maintaining participants' attention as they may have distractions in their environment; and

- the need to establish rapport when interacting online.

Overcoming these challenges requires collaborative planning, clear data management, extensive documentation (Jones et al., 2023) and careful consideration of methodological and ethical issues that may arise (Roberts et al., 2021).

Considering mode and tools for online interview

The decision about which tool to use for online research is not just a technical decision – it requires that the functionality of a given tool or platform aligns with the purposes of the research. The choice of tool or platform will constrain or enable communication and the data that can be generated. A strong alignment between the tool selected and the research focus leads to positive interaction and rich communication.

At its heart qualitative research is about communication between the researcher and the research participants, like any other communication this requires that information and meaning be exchanged in both directions. Online technologies offer a myriad of ways of communicating including email, SMS, blogs, social media apps, audio and video conferencing, virtual worlds and a myriad of other applications. Most internet communication tools can be repurposed for online research, presenting the researcher with a wide range of options.

One way of reducing the options is to consider how the interview is to be conducted. Will it be synchronous or asynchronous? Will the interview be text based or audio/video based? Will it involve multimedia stimulus tools? Will they be conducted one-on-one or as a group interview or focus group? The answers to these questions narrow the options. Other things to consider are the collection and storage of data, data privacy and the terms and conditions of the application being utilized. These latter factors are explored in more detail in Chapters 2 and 3.

Synchronous or asynchronous?

If researchers are seeking to transfer existing methodologies to the online environment, it is likely that they will gravitate to synchronous methods. The opportunity to conduct interviews in real time has the potential to create something that borrows from many of the techniques and approaches associated with face-to-face interviewing or focus groups. Numerous researchers attest to the efficacy of online synchronous interviews (Kite & Phongsavan, 2017; Matthews et al., 2018; Willemsen et al., 2022). However, these interviews, whether one-on-one or group, require familiarity with the technology by the researcher and participants to succeed.

Asynchronous interviews, such as those conducted over time by email, offer an opportunity to collect rich, thoughtful data elicited over a longer timeframe, allowing for reflection from participants (Fritz & Vandermause, 2018). Asynchronous methods include discussion boards, closed email discussions and direct messaging on social media platforms. Many participants will be very familiar with asynchronous communication methods from their own use of a variety of social technologies. Asynchronous methods offer participants a perceived identity shield, which can facilitate an openness to discuss sensitive topics, mitigate social inhibition and provide participants time to ponder the questions put to them (Tuttas, 2015).

Text or multimedia based?

Text-based tools can be attractive to researchers as they avoid the need for costly and time-consuming transcription. Text-based tools can be equalizing as they avoid communication issues that may arise through disability, such as hearing impairment; they can mitigate concerns about appearance and offer less contextual information about socio-economic status, ethnicity, gender, nationality and disability as well as offering actual or perceived anonymity to participants (Tuttas, 2015).

Text-based interviews such as email interviews can increase access to participants, enable participation of working adults, give participants more control over their level of participation and, in some cases, participants have reported enjoying writing about their life experiences (Hawkins, 2018). However, text-based tools are dependent on the researcher's and participants' ability to process information and type quickly (Tuttas, 2015), in the context of synchronous text-based interviews this can place a high cognitive load on participants (Wilkerson et al., 2014). Additionally, the use of text-based tools means that information that can be conveyed through in-person or though multimedia is lost – nodding, body language, verbal agreement (Adams-Hutcheson & Longhurst, 2017). The dependence on text brings with it the need to seek clarification of participants' meaning. In some cases, verbal cues can be compensated through using emoticons and text-speak acronyms such as LMAO (laughing my arse off) but there are clearly cultural and subcultural conventions and associations that may not be shared by all involved in the research, including the researcher who may need to ask for clarification around culturally specific acronyms and paralinguistic expressions.

Video conferencing provides an alternative to text-based research methods. With the ready availability of cloud-based video software such as Skype or Zoom, the use of video conferencing for interviews has become more routine (Archibald et al., 2019; Howlett, 2022; Krouwel et al., 2019) and is considered a valuable qualitative method (Lobe et al., 2022; Lobe & Morgan, 2021). Even with the accessibility of video conferencing software some researchers suggest that audio-only interviews remain especially useful for working with vulnerable populations, and for interviews focused on sensitive topics, such as sexual identity (Heath et al., 2018; Sipes et al., 2022).

Video interviewing has been shown to generate rich data like that produced in face-to-face interviews and focus groups (Abrams et al., 2015; Thunberg & Arnell, 2022). Video conferencing software, such as Zoom, provides the opportunity to add multimedia stimulus materials to the interview. The sharing of images, videos, music and so on, can potentially enrich the communication and generate more data for analysis (Gray et al., 2020). Emerging virtual reality applications offer alternative photorealistic experiences focusing on what participants are seeing and hearing (Mathysen & Glorieux, 2021) and are an alternate means of conducting a multimedia-based interview.

Other considerations for selecting online interview tools

There are several other factors that researchers may wish to think through when considering how they will conduct online interviews and focus groups. The following points are designed to help researchers think through potential issues.

- **Ease of use:** How easy is the tool to use, and what degree of familiarity are researchers and participants likely to have with this tool? A commonly used tool such as email or a social media app is likely to present few technical problems, but it may carry cultural baggage associated with the way such a tool is usually used.

- **Online environment:** Does the tool or online space convey a particular institution or organizational brand? Online spaces convey meaning to participants and so, for example, the use of an educational Virtual Learning Environment (VLE) will position the interview or focus group differently than if it were to take place in a Facebook environment.

- **Data management:** How is the data recorded, saved and managed? It is essential to work out how data will be recorded. Many tools and online environments offer the opportunity to transcribe and/or record sessions. How and where are these recordings saved and how will the researcher access them? Who else might have access to this data?

- **Privacy protections:** How are confidentiality and anonymity ensured? Researchers need to be aware of what research data will be publicly available (perhaps through profiles that are created for the research) and what is collected by the tool that is being used (for example, are IP addressed being recorded)?

- **Resource availability:** What are the financial and other resource issues associated with the use of specific tool? Selection of software or tools may involve real costs (such as subscription) or necessitate the researchers and participants installing software or plug-ins in order to participate in the research.

It is essential that researchers familiarize themselves with potential online tools or environments prior to committing to using them in their research.

Participant selection and recruitment

Many of the challenges associated with participant selection and recruitment in relation to online interviews and focus groups are like those experienced by onsite researchers. Participant selection in qualitative research is approached differently from quantitative research as there is less emphasis on securing a representative sample. Participant selection in qualitative research requires the intentional selection of participants, based on 'criteria that the researcher identifies (either at the beginning or during the course of research) as important to the research question' (Fujii, 2018, p. 38). However, even with this consideration the discussion about sampling in Chapter 4 is also relevant in the context of online interviewing. In essence, the question is whether the use of online methods excludes any individuals or groups or makes individuals more or less likely to want and to be able to participate or to participate fully.

Many online researchers use the internet as a key element of their recruitment strategy, and this will impact the characteristics of the participants that are recruited. Care needs to be taken in the selection strategy to avoid recruitment bias. It can be useful to use a range of tools to interview hard-to-reach populations to offer people multiple options for participation and work with tools that they are comfortable with (Harvey et al., 2023; Heath et al., 2018). Online researchers need to attend to available information about participants' access to technology and their levels of digital literacy during the design of the recruitment and selection process.

A key aspect of the recruitment process is the securing of consent from participants. Onsite norms (information statements, consent forms, verbal explanation and signature) do not work as well in the shift to online. Whether hardcopy forms are required or not, it remains important that participants are informed about the research and their role in it, have the opportunity ask questions and clarify concerns and that this process is recordable and evidencable in some way. The form of this process (whether it be an online form, an email trail or a recording of a discussion) is less important that the fact that the process takes place.

Setting up for success

Interviews and focus groups depend on the establishment of communication between researcher and participants. This is largely dependent on rapport or building a working relationship (Fujii, 2018) and the creation of an atmosphere in which participants want to be involved in the research. Building rapport can be a key component in the success of qualitative research; however onsite techniques may need to be thought about differently in the context of online research (de Villiers et al., 2021). The tool being used for the research may offer opportunities for rapport or relationship building, raising the following questions:

- Does the environment offer opportunities for the sharing of profile pictures among participants?

- Does it offer features that participants can use to convey emotions or ideas in paralinguistic ways, such as with emojis?

- Does the environment allow for formalized turn-taking or direct messaging of a single participant?

Researchers should consider the functionality of the online environment to explore the possibilities for rapport building, management of the group and facilitation of communication. Hugentobler (2022) used emojis and informal language to build rapport with the participants in her Instagram interview.

When working with participants the researcher will need to ensure that the interview functions in a way that is useful for the research. This can sometimes be difficult as the agenda and expectations of participants will not always match that of the researcher. In onsite interviews, researchers can manage the environment and shape the conduct of the interview. The way the furniture is arranged and the modelling of expected behaviour for the conduct of the interview (turn-taking, eye contact, not interrupting others, etc.)

can convey information to participants about how to engage. When interviewing online such strategies need to be rethought. The following suggestions might be employed by the researcher to help manage online interviews and focus groups:

- **Setting expectations:** Beginning interviews with an explicit discussion about the purpose and format of the interviews can be useful in shaping behaviour during the interview.

- **Etiquette:** (Netiquette or Zoom Etiquette). It can be helpful to remind participants, especially in the context of group interviews, of the expected communicative norms in the interview, such as the use of the 'hand up' icon in Zoom to indicate their wish to speak.

- **Prepared responses:** It can be useful to have materials prepared to help the interview flow. This can be pre-prepared stimulus materials (such as a YouTube clip) to get a discussion started or a list of agreed behaviours to deal with challenging behaviour by reminding participants of what was decided.

- **Sending individual messages:** Many discussion tools allow the researcher to message a single participant during a group discussion. This can be used to clarify meaning, check in on participants if they seem distressed or to address problem behaviours.

- **Follow-up contact:** In online environments it is not uncommon for researchers to have to deal with participants who just vanish. They may have left because of technical problems, because they were unexpectedly interrupted; they may have lost interest or objected to the actions of someone else in the interview. For researchers this can be troubling. It can be useful to message participants to follow up with them about the reasons for their departure.

Analysis

In many ways, the analysis of data collected during online research is the same as the analysis of other types of qualitative data and is dependent upon the theories, epistemology and analytic frame being utilized in the research. A big advantage of online interviews is the default production of full-text transcripts or video recordings of the interviews (although such automatic transcripts can still be prone to error). It is important to bear in mind that the interview medium will shape the nature of the communication between researcher and participants and the types of data collected. The nature of the data being gathered has a relationship to the way in which it was gathered, and the analysis will need to reflect this and explore the implications. There are several factors that researchers might wish to attend to as they embark on data analysis.

- **Inaccuracies:** Automatically generated transcripts are generally littered with errors and spelling mistakes. In research with international participants, some accents are not interpreted with the same degree of accuracy as other accents.

- **Context:** To what degree should the analysis take account of the physical location and life context from which the data have been generated? Hugentobler (2022) suggests that the combination of online and onsite data is increasingly necessary as the demarcation between online and offline lives is increasingly blurred.

- **Conversational flow and breaks:** How does the altered structure of the conversational flow (technologically mediated in video interviews and prolonged and broken in asynchronous) affect the nature of the data generated and its analysis? How should the analysis attend to silence and pause in transcript data – these may not hold the same meanings as when they occur in a face-to-face interview. Silences may reflect technical glitches or the difficulties of communicating in a technologically mediated environment.

- **Alignment:** How does the alignment between the online technology being utilized for the research and the research focus impact the data that was collected. For example, conducting interviews on WhatsApp with young people about their social media use (Gibson, 2022) is likely to yield different results than could be obtained through in-person interviews.

In summary

Like all research, to be successful online interviews and focus groups need to represent an appropriate method to answer the research question being asked. When there is alignment between the affordances of the technology being used and the phenomenon under investigation online interviews or focus groups can be especially useful.

The use of online qualitative methods can ameliorate problems caused by cost, geographic distance or time zones and allow for relatively effortless inclusion of dispersed research participants and multimedia stimulus material. Such methods rely on technological knowledge and skills of both researcher and participants so using applications that both are likely to be familiar with is helpful.

Given the rapid technological development and changing social applications (such as social media and emerging virtual meeting sites) researchers need to be reflexive in their approach and learn from their experience, the experience of others (including participants) and adapt to changing social and technological norms and environments.

Further reading

Several resources in the multimedia collection *Sage Research Methods: Doing Research Online* (https://methods.sagepub.com/doing-research-online) offer guidance for the conduct of online group interviews, including Shelton and Jones' (2022) contribution 'Advantages of and considerations for conducting online focus groups'; 'Conducting online focus groups: Challenges and opportunities' (Tremblay et al., 2022); and '"You're on mute": A reflective case study of conducting scenario-based online focus groups on student privacy in higher education' (Jones et al., 2023). Other helpful papers include Janet Salmons' (2015) 'Designing and conducting research with online interviews'; 'Internet interviewing' (James & Busher, 2014); 'Online focus groups' (Abrams & Gaiser, 2016); 'The pedagogy of interviewing' (Roulston, 2012); and 'Interviewing in virtual worlds: The application of best practices' (Cabiria, 2015). A further useful qualitative method is *Social Media Scroll Back Method* (Robarts & Lincoln, 2019).

CHAPTER SIX

Online ethnographies

Ethnography is a research approach that has long been used to understand the daily practice of communities and cultures. Ethnography is used 'to describe and analyse the lives, social worlds, and/or cultures of a group of people in a particular place at a particular time' (Hart, 2017, p. 1) often from the perspective of group members themselves. Online ethnography also termed netnography, virtual ethnography, cyber-ethnography or digital ethnography, can involve traditional ethnographic methods that incorporate digital or online tools in data collection, or ethnographic research undertaken in online or digital spaces, or ethnographies that seek to understand a daily practice that involves online activities (Duggan, 2017; Hine, 2017). The interaction between the social and the technological forms a key concept which defines online ethnographies. This chapter outlines key issues online ethnographers will need to consider when the shift to online complicates traditional ethnographic tenets.

Those new to ethnographic research may like to read this chapter along with an introductory text such as Gobo and Molle's (2016) *Doing Ethnography*, Atkinson's (2022) *Crafting Ethnography*, or *Ethnography Explorations* by Whitaker and Atkinson (2023). Kirner and Mills' texts *Introduction to Ethnography* (2019b) and, the more practically oriented *Doing Ethnographic Research* (2019a) may be useful as well. As ethnography refers to both a research method (fieldwork) and a genre of writing it is also worth reading a range of ethnographic writing to understand the available approaches. The *Journal of Contemporary Ethnography* showcases a variety of ethnographic writing (from online and offline research) and provides coverage of methodological considerations as well.

Case study: An ethnographic study of drug dealing on social media in Nordic countries

To investigate drug dealing on public online platforms, Demant et al. (2019) undertook an online ethnographic study that sought to compare social media drug dealing across the Nordic countries; Norway, Denmark, Sweden, Finland and Iceland. The in-depth ethnographic study found a high degree of drug dealing activity on Facebook, Instagram, Snapchat and Facebook messenger, although there were national differences in the degree of activity and preferred platforms. To undertake the study the research team conducted drug related searches on numerous social media platforms. Upon finding that Facebook and Instagram were most used for drug dealing in three countries, the researchers decided to focus on these platforms. Facebook searches led to public drug-related posts, which led to information about groups, and group invitations to sales and drug discussion groups. Entering groups led to invitations to other groups. On Instagram searches about drugs led to finding public and private profiles associated with people who sell and/or buy drugs. The data collected by the researchers consisted of screenshots of group information, discussions and posts by sellers, buyers and group admins.

Given that the much buying and selling of drugs occurs via private one-to-one messenger-style apps Demant et al. needed to supplement the data obtained through observation (which allowed for the identification of potential informants/participants) with interview data to better understand social media drug dealing. They interviewed 107 participants, although the research team contacted over 100 identified buyers or sellers before getting any willing interviewees. This is typical for hidden population studies.

Demant et al.'s research found that social media in all Nordic countries is being used to deal drugs but with national variation depending on cultural norms about drug use and perception of risk. They argue for increased prevention campaigns to educate people about the risks and consequences of drug use in online settings, rather than increased policing.

Issues highlighted

Demant et al.'s (2019) research shows the limits to participant observation in the online context. Although the team were immersed in social media sites, they could only identify buyers and sellers, the transactional practices were not observable in this context. The ethnographic observations needed to be supplemented with interviews for better understanding of how social media was being used for drug dealing. Møller and Robards (2019) note the ephemeral nature of much online consumption, observable digital traces are not always left so researchers have to find alternative methods to investigate more deeply. Ethnographic methods often incorporate data elicitation techniques, and in this study, this was necessary to get information about participants' actions and their perceptions about risk and the potential consequences of these actions.

Demant et al. needed participants' trust for interviews to take place. Using an encrypted app, Wickr, that was trusted by participants helped. The interviews were conducted asynchronously and lasted between half an hour and two months. Having gained participants' trust, the researchers needed to ensure that their anonymity and privacy were maintained. Ethics approval was obtained at one of the researcher's institutions, but an ethics committee in each of the countries involved was consulted. All interviewees were informed about the study's aims and data management plan. The anonymity of the researchers and interviewees was ensured by the use of Wickr, and the phones used for study were cleaned and reset once data collection had finished. Given the nature of this study, the researchers needed to consider their own safety as well as the ethical obligations that they had towards their participants.

The complexity of online ethnography is illustrated in this study. The research team explored a variety of social media platforms to locate where drug dealing on social media was taking place. They collected data from a variety of sources. They revealed themselves as researchers when recruiting participants for interview but not during the observation phase of the research. To do so then would be to risk being blocked from the group pages where their observations were taking place. Online ethnography allowed for the research to take place unobtrusively in the exploration and observation phases. The phased nature (exploring multiple social media platforms; narrowing the focus to specific social media sites; participant observation; participant identification, recruitment and interviewing) of the research demonstrates the processual, iterative nature of online ethnographic research and the need for a reflexive approach which includes documentation of the decisions made and the reasons behind the decisions.

Ethnographic methods

Ethnographic methods are eclectic and utilize a wide variety of research strategies. While ethnographic research can involve data elicitation methods such as interview, survey or focus groups, ethnography usually includes fieldwork which can take the form of involvement in a group, or at a minimum a lengthy observation, typically participant observation, of the community under study. As a central goal of ethnographic research is to describe cultures and cultural practices (Paoli & D'Auria, 2021), participant observation is considered essential for understanding the difference between what people do and what they say they do (Boellstorff, 2012).

Triangulation or capturing data from multiple sources to increase the validity of interpretation of the data is frequently a feature of ethnographies. In addition to data (such as fieldnotes, photos, audio and/or video recordings, research diaries and so on) gathered through fieldwork ethnography may involve one or more of the following:

- **Interviews** (including group interviews or focus groups);

- **Surveys** which could be quantitative, qualitative or both;

- **Network analysis** (such as observing and recording relationships in a family or community);

- **Topographic** observation and analysis;

- Examination and **analysis of documents**, written and print cultural artifacts;

- Observation; and

- **Historical** and archival analysis.

Ethnographic research is defined, therefore, not by the use of a specific research method or data collection strategy but by a methodological approach that is interpretivist, holistic, embedded in a specific place, highly contextual and conducted over the long term by a researcher embedded in the environment (Hart, 2017).

Digital technologies provide ethnographic researchers with new tools for capturing, preserving and analysing data that supplement traditional processes, new timescales for data collection (a long immersion in an online environment is not necessary for the collection of a large amount of data), as well as new sites for the investigation of cultural practices and meaning making within communities. Such communities can be wholly online or offline communities that use digital tools to connect and communicate.

Online ethnographies

Online ethnography allows researchers to carry out research at low cost across diverse geographic and virtual locations, with dispersed populations (Seligmann & Estes, 2020). Undertaking ethnographic research with digital tools and/or in online settings can complicate some of the key tenets of ethnography. For example, 'culture is no longer considered as strictly linked to physical places but as a flexible construct which can be understood in the different physical and online spaces where meanings are negotiated' (Paoli & D'Auria, 2021, p. 244). Similarly, defining the 'field' where fieldwork is undertaken can be a little more complex with research sites such as podcasts (Lundström & Lundström, 2021), social media apps (Møller & Robards, 2019), instant messaging apps (Käihkö, 2020) or a livestreaming service (Johnson & Woodcock, 2019). The ability to observe or collect data from online communities unobtrusively (such as through lurking or data scrapping) in ways which do not have an onsite equivalent, means that highly contextual and rich data can be collected without requiring 'the continuous and attentive presence' of the researcher (Hart, 2017, p. 1). Online research changes the available parameters of observational and participatory approaches (Costello et al., 2017; Kozinets, 2022; Oreg & Babis, 2023), and it can encompass the study of non-human agents, such as algorithms (Christin, 2020; Lugosi & Quinton, 2018). There is a broad range of data sources available to supplement fieldwork data, and researchers need to consider how much media will be spanned and whether their study will be multi-sited, multi-method and/or multi-modal (Hine, 2017). The following sections of this chapter consider these issues in more depth.

Defining the 'field' in digital fieldwork

With the affordances of online technologies and digital spaces, fieldwork in digital ethnographies is no longer defined (or confined) by geographic or ethnic criteria. The notion of what constitutes a 'field' changes with the online context. A 'field' can be a 'contextual field' such as a blog, discussion forum or Facebook group; contextual fields are 'bounded spaces that bring together people who address a specific audience through a given definition of the situation that gives shape to their social behaviours' (Paoli & D'Auria, 2021, p. 261). This contrasts with a 'meta-field' which rather than being a study of a particular online space, is a study of people involved with a particular online topic. That is, a meta-field is 'a field made up of other fields' where dispersed online activity and communications is united through a shared domain (e.g. a tag or hashtag), 'classified in metadata and created by the daily practices of users who constantly produce social media feeds, search keywords on search engines, use tags and hashtags in this way interacting in a communicative field without space' (Paoli & D'Auria, 2021, p. 261).

Thus, a digital ethnography examining the #MeToo movement (a social movement that went viral in 2017 aiming to reduce sexual abuse by raising awareness of how commonly it occurs through the sharing of stories on social media using the #MeToo hashtag) could use the meta-field created by the #MeToo hashtag as the site of ethnographic research. Paoli and D'Auria (2021) suggest the use of the term 'site' as a substitute for 'field'. Site is a flexible construct spanning different media types and places where cultural activities and meaning making are found. The diversity of potential online research sites allows for the exploration of diverse practices and the emergence of new forms of online ethnography. For example:

- Lundström and Lundström (2021) investigated white radical nationalism through an ethnographic exploration of podcasts, in a process they termed 'podcast ethnography';

- Käihkö (2020) explored the relations between Ukrainian volunteer militias through 'chatnography' by collecting data on social media and instant messaging apps;

- Johnson and Woodcock (2019) used online and onsite ethnographies to explore the impact of livestreaming on the video games industry;

- Kozinets (2022) advocates the use of immersive technologies (such as VR, AR and the Metaverse) to undertake service experience research, through 'immersive netnography'; and

- Brooker (2022) explores the notion of 'computational ethnography' and Lugosi and Quinton (2018) advocate for the use of 'more-than-human' ethnography.

Participation and immersion in online communities

Online ethnography allows for the researcher to be an unobtrusive observer in many online contexts. This can allow for covert observation and data collection. Although there are ethical arguments for and against covert research (see Chapter 3), the case can be made that some research would not be able to take place if the research were revealed to participants. Paoli and Masullo (2022) undertook an online ethnography of the asexual community on Asexual Visibility and Education Network (AVEN – the largest community website for those who self-identify as asexual) to explore the implications of asexuality on identity and society. Paoli and Masullo chose to lurk on AVEN – to covertly access the website and observe users without informing them of their presence nor the research taking place. They argued that for their study a non-participatory approach was preferable as their presence was likely to be unwelcome and undesired by the community. They state, 'in this case the benefits of lurking outweigh the social and ethical costs of such violation' (Paoli & Masullo, 2022, p. 159) and maintain that not announcing their presence allowed for the collection of natural data. They protected users' privacy by reporting quotes anonymously and deleting personal details of users from their data. Sensitive topics are often investigated through observation rather than active participation, such as Menzie's (2022) ethnographic investigation of the online 'incel' movement (men who consider themselves to be involuntarily celibate); or Lavis and Winter's (2020) social media study of peer support for self-harm.

Participant observation (rather than covert observation) is typically a feature of ethnographic research. Participatory approaches allow for participant crosschecks and meaning verification (Thompson et al., 2021) and allow for cocreation in online communities (Costello et al., 2017). Although Thompson et al. (2021) advocate active participation in the field, they suggest an initial period of lurking to understand the norms of the environment prior to getting involved. Once researchers have decided to participate in the online context that they are studying, the question becomes how active or immersed they should be. To be inactive is to risk invisibility in an online community, yet researchers won't want to be leading the community either – there is a risk of distorting the research and biasing the data.

Underwood (2017) describes setting up a Facebook profile, making and responding to posts, posting selfies, watching and responding to thirty-six hours of YouTube videos, and making 'friends' (many of whom became interviewees) in the Zyzz fandom. Zyzz was a recreational bodybuilder (now deceased) who built a large social media following through the creation of an online persona. Underwood's participation in the Zyzz fandom was to learn about participants' views on image and performance-enhancing drugs. While Underwood was actively participating in the Zyzz fandom they maintained an etic, or outsider, perspective. There are strong traditions of emic, or insider perspective being associated with ethnographic methods, which allows online ethnographers to 'view members of the field site not as objects of study but as agential partners in the research venture whose input and perspectives are critically important' (Hart, 2017, p. 4). The emic tradition requires a high degree of immersion in the site of online ethnography.

Fieldnotes are an essential feature of ethnography. Fieldnotes are data that provides a record of what the researcher did, what happened as a result, what was learnt and how the researcher experienced it. The experiential elements of online participation or observation (where you do it, how you feel, what devices you used) are all part of the ethnographic process (Hart, 2017) and researchers should carefully consider how they will document this. Techniques like reflective journals or blogs are good ways to capture this data. Researchers may wish to consider carefully how their own emotional, social and intellectual journeys can be captured and incorporated into the process of analysis and presentation. Online autoethnography focuses on the embodied experience of the online researcher and is emerging as an important source of insight in its own right (Hine, 2017).

Triangulation and research scope

Ethnographic research rarely rests on the use of observational or participatory data, often other forms of data are gathered during the research process. There is a wide range of data types that can inform online ethnographies; some of which could include those drawn from the visual methods tradition (Udupa, 2019), or the collection of archival or elicited data. Archival data, which can include big data (Laaksonen et al., 2017), describes naturally occurring data that the researcher has accessed for the purpose of the study. Data mining methods are being used with digital archives, offering opportunities for new analysis (Barnes et al., 2022; Mockler, 2020a). Naturally occurring data can be captured and recorded through a variety of means (such as screen shotting, data scrapping, audio or visual recording, etc.), enabling collection of data from blogs, Twitter/X, social media posts, message boards, YouTube, podcasts and many other online applications. Where data is publicly available, some researchers might argue that there is no reason to treat it differently from other public media; however, in general, the consensus is that a situated ethical approach should be taken, with factors such as users' expectation of privacy, vulnerability, the purpose and benefits of research to be considered (franzke et al., 2020). Chapter 3 provides a full discussion of ethics in the context of online research.

Data can be elicited in participatory research by asking participants for clarification in a discussion or requesting more information. Other methods of eliciting data, such as interviews and surveys, are discussed at greater length in Chapters 4 and 5. Archer interviewed 'Mummy' bloggers to learn why they blogged during her online ethnography of influencer culture (Archer, 2019); and in her ethnography of music in algorithmic culture Werner (2020) interviewed eighty young people about music consumption through platforms such as Spotify.

In the context of ethnographic research, elicited and archival data is often used as a means of triangulation. Triangulation is a process used to increase the reliability and validity of research findings by combining different data collection methods and different sources of data to verify and cross-check the accuracy of data and its interpretation. This approach helps to reduce the biases that may occur when relying on a single method, such as observation, or a single source of data, such as archival or elicited data. By comparing different sources of data, the researcher can gain a more comprehensive understanding of a community and its culture (Angelone, 2019). Triangulation is one approach to the problem of gauging authenticity online. The authenticity of an individual's online claims or identity may be difficult to determine, given that identity is performed differently online to onsite (Hine, 2017).

In addition to incorporating a range of data sources in their research, the researcher has a variety of models available for conducting online ethnography. Hine (2017, p. 10) classifies them in the following ways:

- **Online:** The ethnographer studies activities within some online space (or connected set of spaces) on their own terms, without seeking to situate those activities within offline spaces.

- **Multi-modal:** Different communication modes (potentially including face-to-face communication, documents, telephone, social networking sites and other online spaces) are studied because they are used by an identifiable group of people who form the focus of the study.

- **Multi-sited:** A set of interconnected sites is identified, either in advance of the study or as the study progresses, as offering insights into different facets of the experience of interest.

- **Blended:** A study which combines two (or more) approaches – often online and offline observation to explore a given phenomenon. The actual form of the blending varies, possibly involving a structured comparison between the two approaches, or possibly a more dynamic blending involving the ethnographer moving between sites as in a networked, multi-sited or connective approach.

- **Networked:** A set of interconnections is followed by the ethnographer by tracing the flow of communication between a group of people or activity of interest. New sites may emerge in a dynamic fashion in the course of the study, rather than being identified in advance.

- **Connective:** The ethnographer moves between different modes of communication and locations (online or offline) according to a set of theoretically driven interests focusing on the contingent connections that emerge as people appropriate and make sense of online activities offline and vice versa (also referred to as hybrid ethnography).

With the intricacy of people's use of an array of onsite and online services, apps, websites and communication methods it can be difficult to define and bound the research site(s) that form the basis of an online ethnographic study. The range of models above speaks to the complexity of attempting to capture the activities of participants. Additionally, the ability to collect a large volume of data rapidly challenges traditional notions of temporality in ethnography (Tunçalp & Lê, 2014). The research aims and focus will shape the scope of the project, and in some cases the research process undertaken will situate the study. In the case study discussed at the start of this chapter, Demant et al. (2019) defined the research site by investigating several social media sites and then confining the research to the two social media sites found to be most useful to the research. This narrowed the scope of the project making data collection (and therefore storage and analysis) more manageable. Bounding the study is not the only issue that needs to be managed; online researchers also need to consider the ethical, methodological and technical challenges that come with online ethnography.

Ethics and other challenges of online ethnographies

As noted, online ethnography brings with it ethical challenges (Hair et al., 2023; Thompson et al., 2021). Decisions about lurking versus active participation and whether, when and how to reveal the research project have clear ethical implications. Researchers also need to attend to participant vulnerability, right to privacy and anonymity; informed consent; how data will be stored and protected; researcher safety; the potential of harm or benefit of the research; and the requirements of their institution's ethics review board. The situated nature of ethnography suggests the need for ethical pluralism, careful consideration of the particularities of the research project and a process for documenting the ethical decisions made, the justification for these and any ethical tensions that were experienced during the research (franzke et al., 2020).

The complexity of the online environment poses methodological challenges beyond the selection of a suitable ethnographic model. Changes in the structure of the internet, its increasing reliance on platforms (Srnicek, 2016), or digital enclosures (Andrejevic, 2022), mean that researchers can find it harder to access data from social media sites and other online apps. The way that these platforms use algorithms to manipulate the experience of participants also means that researchers need to be aware that their experience and observations of the field will be filtered through an algorithmic lens meaning that what they see may be different from what others see.

As discussed in Chapter 2 the prevalence of big data brings new data collection methods, which can supplement the data collected through observation or elicitation (Laaksonen et al., 2017). However, such methods hold technical challenges. Online ethnography involves mastery of particular technologies, not just of the platform where data is collected (such as social media sites, virtual worlds or messenger apps) but also technologies for the recording, scrapping, storage, analysis and presentation of data.

Undertaking online ethnographic study

How researchers approach their online research and its participants will depend on both their methodological approach and the research aims. While generalization is difficult, the following suggestions might be helpful for building trust and engagement:

- Learn the affordances of and how to use the technologies being employed in the research, including those that will be used for the management of the data collected in the study.

- Take time to find out about the communities you are entering before you announce your project. This will give you some insights about how to avoid offending or confusing people.

- Be aware that attempts to enter communities and provision of information about research projects (however worthwhile) may be perceived as intrusion or spamming. This is particularly the case in communities that have been researched before, especially if that experience was not positive for the community.

- Consider whether you want to lurk (watch without participating) before you announce your presence and whether you will be collecting data while lurking. There are ethical issues to consider in lurking, but it is likely to enable you to judge the appropriate tone of an initial post and subsequent participation.

- Enable (potential) participants to find out further information about your project and research aims – perhaps by directing them to a website, blog or YouTube video. Avoid deluging people with information at the initial point of contact and use accessible language in your communication with people.

- Think about how much time, disclosure and engagement you require from participants, especially in your first approach. Participants are more likely to be engaged if trust is first established through small interactions, prior to more substantial requests for time/communication/engagement are made.

As this chapter has described, online ethnographic research is multi-method and multi-modal. It requires reflexivity, careful planning and data management and analysis skills. The process of bringing together a range of different and sometimes contradictory findings is a key skill of the ethnographer. While this challenge is not confined to online research, online research can frequently lead to the proliferation of different data types and the rapid accumulation of what can be very large data sets. Researchers may find themselves faced with masses of text, images, audio, video, maps of networks and the outputs of an array of other ways in which individuals and communities present themselves and interact online.

With a large corpus of data, data analysis in ethnographic research can be complex. While there are challenges associated with the accumulation of large amounts of data through online research, it is important to remember that the online environment offers a wide range of tools, such as CAQDAS, which can aid ethnographic processes, such as the mapping of networks, options for sophisticated data visualization, the coding of qualitative data, searching through large data sets and so on. Some forms of computer-assisted representation and analysis of data are discussed further in Chapters 2 and 9.

While a much fuller discussion of the process of analysis of online ethnographic data is possible (see the further reading section below), the following may be a useful starting point for planning a suitable analytical approach:

- Consider your approach to anonymity of the data carefully. Researchers especially working in closed communities or with vulnerable populations have a responsiblity to protect the participants (Wang & Liu, 2021). Quoted phrases can be located using search engines and the use of participants' screen names does not protect anonymity as users frequently employ the same screen name across a variety of platforms and these can be as recognizable as a given name.

- Consider the approach to data archiving before embarking on research. While it can be tempting to consider the web as an online repository, it is important to recognize that there are limits to search and recall technologies, and websites are not permanent (Angelone, 2019). Are you going to use CAQDAS? If so, how will you get your data into it?

- Consider what kind of coding approach you are going to use and how this will be derived from your data as the project unfolds.

- Think about how open your data analysis is going to be. Will you consult participants about the codes you are using or the findings that you are generating?

- Consider what audiences your findings will be disseminated to and in what forms (see Chapter 8 for a discussion about this). For example, it is common practice to not just provide a research report and publish in academic forms but also use a blog to present project findings and reflections on the process to participants, stakeholders and other researchers.

In summary

Online ethnographic research provides a powerful approach for investigating human experience, activity and interaction and changed nature of human relationships through digital technologies. While the online/onsite distinction is becoming less clear, connective, blended and hybrid ethnographies offer researchers a way to document and analyse the increased integration of digital technologies into people's lives. Researchers who use ethnographic methods need to recognize the conceptual and organizational complexity of human relationships, and to develop approaches that engage with people both online and onsite in multi-method, multi-site and multi-modal ways. Despite the complexity and the challenges (ethical, methodological and technical), there are reasons to be excited about the possibilities offered by online ethnographies. The continued expansion of naturally occurring data alongside the increasing ease of access to powerful computational tools to search and analyse it means ethnographers are faced with a wealth of opportunities for interaction and research with online communities, networks and social movements.

Further reading

There are several useful works that focus on online ethnographic methods. These include *Ethnography for the Internet* (Hine, 2015); *Netnography: The essential guide to qualitative social media research* (Kozinets, 2019); and *Digital Ethnography: Principles and practice* (Pink et al., 2016). Given the increase in ethnographic work that involves study of both online and onsite activity *Hybrid Ethnography: Online, offline and in between* (Przybylski, 2020) is also worth reading.

CHAPTER SEVEN

Online experiments

Researchers undertaking online experiments draw on a rich and longstanding methodological tradition that has been reworked for a new environment. As with other online methods, a key question is how they compare to onsite laboratory and field experiments. There is considerable evidence that online experiments produce similar results to comparable laboratory-based research (Gould et al., 2015; Hergueux & Jacquemet, 2015; Keuschnigg et al., 2016). Although there is some evidence which suggests that there may be minor differences in results which are attributable to mode (Ozono & Nakama, 2022), most observed differences between online and laboratory cohorts are more easily explained by the different characteristics of the cohorts (Lee et al., 2018).

This chapter focuses on exploring when, where and how to use online experiments most effectively for social research.

Experimental methods in the social sciences

Most online social experiments are in the disciplines of psychology or economics, but they can also be found across the social sciences in areas such as political science and marketing as well as in areas such as ergonomics and computer-human interaction which increasingly overlap with the social sciences. It is also worth noting that there are big overlaps with other social science methods. Much of the research cited in Chapter 4 (surveys) is also worth looking at when developing online experiments.

For further information about designing social science experiments, researchers may wish to consult Green's (2022) *Social Science Experiments* or Coleman's (2018) *Designing Experiments for the Social Sciences*. Economists may also be interested in Chaudhuri's (2021) *Behavioural Economics and Experiments* or Duflo and Banerjee's (2017) *Handbook of Field Experiments*. Psychologists might want to consult Harris et al. (2021) *Designing and Reporting Experiments in Psychology* or Maclin's (2020) *Experimental Design in Psychology*.

Case study: An experiment to explore the believability of 'fake news'

There has been substantial debate in contemporary media about the prevalence and believability of 'fake news'. Researchers in Hong Kong were interested to discover whether an individual's ability to identify the validity of online new media was related to their existing political position (Au et al., 2021).

They recruited 398 participants (cleaned down to 380 to remove poor-quality responses) by offering a small incentive (around £5.00) and then administered the experiment through a common online survey tool (LimeSurvey). In the survey tool participants were asked to provide some demographics, information about their political orientation (based on their voting record), media consumption and approach to verifying online information.

Participants were then presented with a series of articles about contemporary political issues in Hong Kong. These were chosen to showcase a range of different political perspectives and to provide a mix of true stories (largely drawn from established media sources) and fake news (largely drawn from content farms and website which do not attribute articles to authors nor provide source information). The original source of all the stories was obscured.

Participants were asked to review fifteen stories and to evaluate their reliability. The data were then analysed statistically to identify patterns in responses. Unsurprisingly they found that those participants who were more aware of misinformation, and who had strategies to combat it, were more likely to be able to identify the fake news. More surprisingly the research found that those further to the political extremes were better at identifying misinformation and that reading a wide range of media did not necessarily improve the ability to identify misinformation.

The researchers argue that their main finding for policy makers is that there is a need to develop media literacy among the population. The study concludes by reflecting on its limitations. It points out that the Hong Kong case may not be generalizable to other political contexts. It also highlights the fact that the sample used in the study lacked diversity in terms of personality types and socio-economic status.

Despite its limitations the experimental approach was able to demonstrate some of the challenges associated with identifying 'fake news' and suggest some evidence-based approaches that could be attempted to try and address this issue.

Key issues raised

This study shows that it is possible to adapt online survey tools to undertake certain types of online experiment. This makes conducting online experiments very accessible as they do not necessarily require any specialist equipment beyond a survey tool.

As with all social science research, decisions about sampling, including the demographics of the participants, need to be made carefully as this will affect the generalizability of the findings. The use of a snowballing approach to sampling combined with a small incentive shaped the sample that was recruited and meant that demographic diversity was limited. However, care was taken to recruit a sufficiently large sample to be able to have confidence in the finding, even if representativeness could not be claimed.

This research shows that online experiments can address contemporary political issues and be of interest to policymakers and the wider political discourse. Au et al. (2021) include a substantial section of their article discussing the implications for contemporary Hong Kong politics, which was a context in which discussion of the functioning of democracy and the role that the media played in this was critical as the country's democracy was under considerable pressure during this period.

Advantages and disadvantages
of experimenting online

As with other online methods, online experiments have several advantages over onsite experiments. It is possible to summarize these advantages as follows:

- **Larger and more diverse samples:** The ability to access large numbers of diverse subjects through the internet has been a boon for experimental research (Sauter et al., 2020). They also allow researchers to conduct experimental research with hard-to-reach populations such as clinical populations.

- **Cheaper, faster and more efficient:** Online experiments can be cheaper than the experimental laboratories and facilities that are traditionally maintained by social scientists. They also allow experimenters to run experiments quickly, with participants engaging in multiple time zones around the clock.

- **Scale up more easily:** Online experiments can be scaled up more easily as researchers can work with larger cohorts (Sauter et al., 2020). At the extremes we would highlight Bond et al. (2012). They conducted a field experiment with sixty-one million American voters using Facebook.

- **Reduce experimenter bias:** Online experiments may also reduce the bias associated with experimenter presence (Crump et al., 2013).

Online experiments also suffer from many of the disadvantages already discussed for other online research methods. These include the following:

- **Technically demanding:** The use of online experiments makes a technical demand on both resperimenters and participants and is reliant on the effective functioning of a range of technologies.

- **Loss of control:** It can be more difficult to control the experience of online participants (Keuschnigg et al., 2016).

Participants could be watching TV, eating and drinking or undertaking any other activity that can be combined with smartphone use (i.e. essentially anything) (Crump et al., 2013).

- **Collusion and cross-talk:** In online experiments it can be more difficult to ensure that cross-talk, collusion and plagiarism does not take place (Lee et al., 2018).

- **Loss of physical presence:** Online experiments make it much more difficult to undertake experiments in which physical proximity, manipulation or measurement are important (Lee et al., 2018). This includes some but not all forms of physiological measurement, for example, eye-tracking studies have become increasingly possible in online environments (Saxena et al., 2022).

- **Non-human actors:** There is also the possibility that some experiments can be completed by non-human actors (bots), particularly where payment accompanies the completion of experiments (Crump et al., 2013). However, it is possible to identify bots and reduce their impact by monitoring geolocation and IP addresses and inserting pre-experimental checks to exclude non-human actors (Moss & Litman, 2018).

A consideration of the advantages and disadvantages suggests that careful and critical use of online experiments is justified. Many of these issues are simply restatements of existing questions of research quality.

Designing online experiments

Online experiments are not a methodology in themselves, but rather a particular mode through which experimental research can be conducted. Researchers are therefore advised to begin from their research questions or themes and to develop a methodological approach in response to this. In some cases, this methodological consideration will lead towards an online approach, while in others it will lead to conventional laboratory or field approaches or to a blended approach.

While there are good reasons to be positive about the value of online experiments, the online environment is clearly not appropriate for all research questions. Online experiments may not offer the most appropriate approach where identity verification, access to populations with low digital literacy or digital access, physical interaction with people or materials or a high level of control over the environment are important. However, such issues are not necessarily solved by conducting the research in a face-to-face environment.

It is also important to be clear that it is possible to combine online and onsite experiments. Wiersma notes that there are several places where the distinction between online and onsite experiments becomes blurred, such as laboratory experiments preceded by an online survey, laboratory experiments validated over several sites, or the use of email as a stimulus for field experiments (Wiersma, 2012). An example of an online/onsite combination is found in Burger et al. who conducted related online and field experiments to explore students' self-control in relation to study behaviour (2011). The field component enabled the researchers to observe students' behaviour, while the online element allowed a larger sample size and more rapid execution of the experiment.

As with other kinds of online research, there are a range of different types of online experiments. It is not possible to discuss all possible types of online experiments here, but we will address several common types to highlight how some of the key issues in online experiments morph as the methodologies and technologies used have changed.

Survey-based research

In many ways survey-based experiments offer some of the most technically simple ways to undertake experimental studies. Survey-based approaches (such as that discussed in the Au et al. (2021) case study above) make use of survey technologies to provide participants with stimulus and then measure their reaction to them.

Survey-based experiments can be a very accessible, efficient and reliable way to undertake experiments, but the quality of the data collected and therefore their generalizability and validity is dependent on both the careful construction and testing of the instrument and on the sample that is recruited (Mullinix et al., 2015).

Time measurement experiments

Some experiments require the measurement of reaction time or some other kind of time sensitive measurement. Technical challenges related to hardware and software performance, connectivity and internet stability can present problems for these kinds of experiments (Sauter, 2020).

To address concerns about the accurate measurement of reaction time over the internet, researchers should identify software that can run these kinds of experiments and collect data that allows for the verification of their validity (Barnhoorn et al., 2015). Most online experimental systems should be able to provide data on their precision as well as providing researchers with the data collected (Sauter et al., 2020).

Despite these concerns about accuracy, there is research showing that online time measurement studies provide comparable results to laboratory-based studies (Kim et al., 2019; Simcox & Fiez, 2014). While specialist laboratory-based reaction time software still offers a more reliable measure, particularly when investigating individual differences, there is good reason to be confident about time measurement data collected online, including responses gathered through smartphones and tablets (De Leeuw & Motz, 2016; Pronk et al., 2020).

Interactive experiments

Interactive experiments describe any experiments in which individuals interact with each other (Arechar et al., 2018). This requires different kinds of technologies to the more individualized kinds of experiments discussed so far. This can be challenging for researchers as it requires additional technical capacity (Hawkins, 2015), but in a world in which video conference and other forms of online collaboration are becoming increasingly commonplace it is usually possible to overcome these technical hurdles.

Arechar et al. (2018) find that the quality of online interactive experiments is similar to laboratory-based experiments. While many of the issues raised in the rest of this chapter in relation to sampling and careful experimental design hold true for interactive experiments, there is broad support for the idea that these types of experiments can be successfully conducted online.

Virtual reality

An important sub-set of online experiments are those that build virtual reality simulated environments. While all virtual reality experiments make use of digital technologies, not all of them use the internet, with some using virtual reality technologies in the laboratory, particularly where it is important to have immersive environments which use specialist technology such as headsets.

Where virtual reality is effectively used it can increase the authenticity of simulations and strengthen the implied context within which such experiments are conducted. Research demonstrates that virtual reality experiments typically give similar findings to those conducted in a laboratory (Innocenti, 2017).

Innocenti (2017) distinguishes between low-immersive virtual environments (LIVE) such as Second Life, World of Warcraft or other screen-based virtual worlds, and high immersive virtual environments (HIVE) which make use of headsets, multiple screens and other technologies to enable the individual to become more fully immersed in the environment. The greater the degree of immersion the more realistic such experiments can become and the greater chance they have of simulating real environments in ways that elicit 'real' behaviour from individuals.

However, while more convincing forms of immersion improve the generalizability of the findings of online experiments, virtual reality tools also allow a range of biases to enter the environment which may mitigate against the wider generalizability of the experiment. For example, in virtual environments in which people can craft their appearance and identity they may be behaving in different ways than they would in a physical environment.

Many commercial virtual reality environments also create an implied political economy in which questions of power, scarcity and authority can vary dramatically from physical world contexts. While the ability to manipulate such fundamental elements of the social world, is one of the key advantages of virtual reality experiments, the level of control afforded to the researcher will vary depending on the tool that is used. These issues need to be carefully reflected on by researchers who are making use of virtual reality.

Field experiments

Field experiments offer researchers the opportunity to conduct experiments in more 'natural' environments which more fully capture contexts (Muise & Pan, 2019). Such field experiments have been extensively conducted in a wide range of online environments (Chen & Konstan, 2015). Field experiments necessarily include a greater range of variables in the experiment which are not fully in the control of the researcher.

Parigi et al. (2017) argue that the development of big data as part of online and blended environments expands the possibilities that are offered by field experiments. An increasing amount of individuals' interaction with the environment is not only recorded but also quantified in ways that support analysis. The fact that an individual who participates in an online experiment can also provide access to their career history, credit score or level of social connectedness simply by consenting to having their data linked to other data source, can provide researchers with new insights as well as new ethical issues.

Online field experiments will typically recruit a sample from the users of an existing website, app or community and assign them to a variety of conditions (e.g. treatment and control). Such an experiment captures people in a real environment and then manipulates some aspect of that environment to explore its effect. For example, a large-scale and controversial study manipulated to the emotional content of the Facebook newsfeeds of almost 700,000 people to see how shifts in emotional content changed the way in which they interacted with Facebook (Kramer et al., 2014). Such studies usually require close collaboration with website, app or platform owners or the ability to use its functionality to access the required population (e.g. buying adverts on sites like Facebook or Google). Data is not just collected on the response to the experiment, but also on the participants' interaction with other elements of the online environment, other people and anything else that is important.

Considering what tools to use

The tools used to undertake online experiments are closely related to the context in which the experiment will be conducted. In many cases, the site that is chosen as the context will also form the experimental tools. For example, an experiment may offer a participant a virtual maze to explore (context), but the researcher will choose a site that enables the accurate recording of participants' behaviour, thus transforming the context into a research tool. In many cases the ability to manipulate the context to suit the needs of the online experiment will be a key requirement of the researcher.

Increasingly, it is possible to find highly configurable environments without needing to buy or purpose-build a site. Being a careful consumer of others' products is probably a more useful skill for the online experimenter than being a programmer. When creating online experiments, researchers are typically looking for a tool that offers some or all the following functionalities:

- **Useable:** Tools need to be easy for researchers to use or learn how to use. Different levels of technical knowledge mean that different researchers will feel comfortable using different tools.

- **Adaptable:** The site needs to offer researchers sufficient flexibility and control to ensure that they can shape it to the experiment's needs.

- **Visible:** Researchers need to be able to see what goes on in their online experiments.

- **Enclosable:** Some experiments may require that researchers can control who has access to the environment and when people have access to it.

- **Recordable:** Most research requires that what takes place in the online environment can be recorded in some way.

- **Analysable:** The online experiment needs to produce data in a format that it is possible for the researcher to analyse.

There are several purpose-built tools that researchers can use for online experiments. A range of bespoke tools have been developed to support researchers who are interested in creating online experimental studies. The iScience server (https://www.iscience.eu/) created by the researcher Ulf-Dietrich Reips provides a very useful guide to pre-existing tools.

Many of the existing sites and tools offer useful functionality that can save your time, but typically they have also made a variety of choices, leaving the experimenter with less freedom than if they create their own environment (Chen & Konstan, 2015). Because of this some researchers might want to develop tools for online experiments themselves. To do this you will need to use a browser-compatible programming language such as JavaScript. Some researchers have created libraries of support, resources and tools to help others to create online experiments.

Additional tools to support the building of online experiments

Gorilla (https://gorilla.sc/)
jsPsych (https://www.jspsych.org/7.3/)
lab.js (https://lab.js.org/)

Whatever tool is selected it is important to understand and to be able to answer questions (for example in ethics applications) about where the experiment and the resulting data is going to be hosted. This decision will raise substantial ethical and data protection issues that need to be fully addressed at the design stage (Sauter et al., 2020).

Managing recruitment

A key challenge in experimental design is creating an experiment that you will be able to get people to undertake and complete. The challenge of recruitment has already been discussed in Chapters 4 and 5 and much of the learning can be transferred over to the area of online experiments.

Recruiting participants is challenging in all experimental studies. The internet opens a vast online pool of participants and it is possible to advertise an online study from a wide range of places, such as Facebook, email lists, blogs, websites, discussion boards and so on. Indeed, the quality of an experimental participant pool can be enhanced by recruiting from multiple sites (Reips, 2007).

Participant motivation

It is useful to think about what motivates participants to engage in online experiments. Many researchers have found that participants are financially motivated and that the provision of small amounts of money can support recruitment.

For economists and others interested in markets, offering a financial incentive, particularly through a real online labour market like MTurk, can be an advantage as it allows for the study of incentive and motivation in a real rather than simulated context (Keuschnigg et al., 2016). For others the marketized nature of such platforms adds an additional ethical concern to their use (Palan & Schitter, 2018; Williamson, 2016). Crump et al. (2013) argue that researchers have an ethical responsibility to pay people a similar amount to what they would if they were delivering the experiment in a laboratory. However, Williamson (2016) argues that paying above the market rate on crowdsourcing sites may distort the sample. She favours providing a retrospective bonus for those who complete the study to bring their compensation up to ethical levels (e.g. the minimum wage) without biasing the sample.

Not everyone active on paid-for platforms such as MTurk is primarily or exclusively motivated by money (Paolacci & Chandler, 2014). Many participants on these sites, as well as those recruited through other platforms and sites, are motivated by a range of non-monetary rewards. Jun et al. (2017) have identified that participants in online experiments are variously motivated by boredom, the desire to compare yourself with others, fun, science and self-learning. Unsurprisingly different kinds of studies work on different motivations. These variations have an impact on the sample that is recruited, how people participate and who drops out.

Researchers should be aware of these motivations while recruiting as actively appealing to them can increase recruitment (August et al., 2018). Appealing to the desire for participants to compare themselves with others or to learn more about themselves are more successful in attracting participants than those which play on more altruistic motivations. There is also some evidence to suggest that experiments that are at least somewhat fun and engaging are likely to be more appealing and lead to better data quality (Crump et al., 2013).

Crowdsourcing platforms

The opportunity to use crowdsourcing platforms, particularly those that offer participants financial compensation has enabled researchers to access new, broader and potentially more international populations than in much traditional experimental research (Keuschnigg et al., 2016; Palan & Schitter, 2018). They also importantly enable experimental researchers to scale up their samples in a cost-effective way.

There has been criticism of paid-for crowdsourced samples with some arguing that they result in different but equally problematic samples to traditional approaches. Crowdsourcing platforms typically over-represent younger and more educated and under-employed participants (Paolacci & Chandler, 2014). Unsurprisingly, the population that can be accessed through this kind of site differs in a range of ways from the general population, both in terms of its demographics and its personality.

Researchers should also be wary of the way in which crowdsourcing platforms, particularly those which pay subjects, can lead to the growth of 'professional experimental subjects' who spend all of their time participating in these kinds of experiments and therefore might be expected to behave in a different way to more typical subjects (Hillygus et al., 2014; Keuschnigg et al., 2016; Palan & Schitter, 2018). Some researchers have referred to this as the problem of 'non-naiveite' (Chandler et al., 2014; Peer et al., 2017). There is not much evidence to suggest that non-naïve participants participate less seriously in research studies than more naïve participants (Hillygus et al., 2014). In fact, they may be more attentive to instructions than conventional subject pools (Hauser & Schwarz, 2016). However, their experience may mean that they participate in a different way, with some studies suggesting that using non-naïve participants will result in smaller effect sizes (Chandler et al., 2015).

Concerns with naivety focus attention on sampling practices used in online surveys. Robinson et al. (2019) argue that researchers are often too swayed by the 'reputations' of workers on crowd sourcing platforms (which purport to offer a measure of their reliability and trustfulness) and that many of the problems with non-naivety can be addressed by actively sampling inexperienced, less active and supposedly less reliable workers on such platforms. Other researchers argue that this can be addressed by making efforts to identify and exclude non-naïve participants through forms of pre-experiment assessment (Chandler et al., 2014).

Similarly, there have been concerns raised about whether the difficulty of verifying identities on crowdsourcing platforms leads to people maintaining multiple accounts and getting paid for participating in the same experiment multiple times. However, research suggests that while this does happen it is relatively rare (Palan & Schitter, 2018).

These concerns have led to the establishment of a plethora of alternatives to MTurk. Some of these recruit on a similar financial basis to MTurk, while others are framed as academic or research tools and participation is on a voluntary basis.

Examples of crowdsourcing platforms

Crowd Flower https://visit.figure-eight.com/People-Powered-Data-Enrichment_T
LabInTheWild https://labinthewild.org/
Otree http://www.otree.org/
Prolific https://www.prolific.co/
Psytoolkit https://www.psytoolkit.org/

The choice of crowd sourcing platform ultimately becomes an important methodological choice, with different platforms offering different possibilities, somewhat different populations, different ethical and technical challenges (Peer et al., 2017).

The following questions may be useful in deciding on which crowd sourcing platform to use:

- Are the rules about rights, responsibilities and payment clear?

- Is it possible to vary the payment and incentive that you offer?

- Is there transparency about the population that you can access through this platform? What kind of pre-screening and verification is offered?

- Is there any way to limit the recruitment of 'professional' research participants?

- What kinds of protections exist to prevent the participation of bots?

- Can you exclude respondents who cause problems or who consistently provide poor-quality data?

- Can you track respondents over time, engage them in multi-stage experiments or recontact them?

- What tools exist for testing your experiment before you go live with it?

- Can it easily be run alongside participants recruited through other platforms or as part of a hybrid experiment?

- What tools exist to allow you to monitor recruitment, attrition and progress in the experiment?

- Can you customize the look and feel of the platform (adding logos, graphics and particular question and game types)?

- What level of technical skills does it require and do these match with your capabilities?

In general, the concerns about crowdsourced samples should not mean that researchers do not use these very useful sources of participants. Rather it is important to be mindful about sample characteristics and to think about the way in which other sampling strategies can be used to allow for triangulation of findings.

Managing experiments

Consent and participant information

As with all forms of research, it is important to provide participants with information about the study that they are participating in and to gain their informed consent. However, experimental researchers have used online experiments to examine how thoroughly participants read such information and concluded that most people pay scant attention to them (Jun et al., 2017). This lack of attention is even greater among younger people and male participants. There is some evidence to suggest that problems parsing participant information and instructions are greater for online experiments than laboratory-based experiments (Gould et al., 2015).

Given this, it is important to test participants' understanding of what they are being asked to do in some way (e.g. a comprehension question that serves as an exclusion criteria) or providing prompts throughout the experiment at appropriate points (Crump et al., 2013). There is also some evidence which suggests that pictorial, step-by-step instructions can be useful in supporting participant understanding (Sauter et al., 2020).

Participant experience and managing dropout

High levels of attrition are a greater concern in online experimental research than in laboratory-based research (Sauter et al., 2020). Participants are free to leave at any time and do not need to give a reason or face any social pressure when they do so. Such attrition, and particularly the fact that it can be patterned by demographics and personality type, has the potential to confound the representativeness of online experiments (Zhou & Fishbach, 2016).

Shorter experiments are less likely to experience dropout (Sauter et al., 2020), with Crump et al., (2013) arguing that it is optimum to keep task length under thirty minutes. Ideally studies should be engaging and, where possible, fun to participate in. Gamification is one strategy through which this can be achieved (Sauter et al., 2020).

Researchers should monitor participants dropout carefully and identify key points at which people drop out (Crump et al., 2013). Dropout should be a subject worthy of analysis, particularly looking at how dropout shapes the characteristics of your sample, with the level and nature of attrition reported and reflected upon (Zhou & Fishbach, 2016).

In summary

As with other online research methods, online experiments offer researchers considerable advantages. The decision to situate an experiment within the online environment is one that must be taken carefully and for sound methodological reasons. However, there are a wide range of advantages in terms of cost, time and improved quality. Online experiments open the possibility for new kinds of studies, in terms of improving the quality of observations, the potential scale of experiments, and the ability to explore a range of topics directly related to the online environment.

Further reading

There are a number of useful texts that can provide a deeper discussion of online experiments, including Gosling and Johnson's (2010) *Advanced Methods for Conducting Online Behavioral Research* and Reips and Buchannan's (2022) *Web-Based Research in Psychology*.

CHAPTER EIGHT

Communicating research online

One of the main questions when you are undertaking a research project is how you are going to communicate what you are doing and what you find. The 'public communication of science' has become an influential agenda for many researchers (Bucci & Trench, 2021), but regardless of whether you are trying to communicate with 'the public', with a small group of people who share your academic interests or with other groups, such as participants and stakeholders in your research, the internet offers new opportunities for making yourself heard.

This chapter focuses on how you can use online technologies, platforms and spaces to aid in the communication of your research. Ultimately it asks you to think through the following questions:

- **Why** do you want to communicate your research?

- **Who** do you want to communicate with?

- **When** do you want to communicate, particularly whether communication starts during the project or only after you have results? and

- **How** are you going to communicate?

Why communicate research?

Research is a social process which involves other people. We read other people's papers, respond to them, undertake research, publish and present and also respond to questions, challenges and critiques. For some researchers this process can be confined to a small group of technical specialists, but for many the implications of their research have consequences for individuals, organizations, products, services, politics or society. In such cases the desire to communicate is likely to be greater and researchers feel a need to communicate more widely.

For social researchers, the need to communicate with others is even greater as people are the subject of their research. In many cases, social researchers will need to communicate the purpose of their research, engage people in it, help them understand how to participate and ultimately provide feedback on what was achieved through the research.

Case study

For this case study we add a brief reflection by the two authors of this book on the way in which they communicate research online.

Tristram Hooley: I am very keen to make sure that the research that I do is read by others. I work in an applied field, and so as well as other researchers, I am keen to reach out and connect with practitioners and policymakers.

The main tool that I use for the communication of my research is my blog. I have been writing this for around fifteen years and use it to communicate opportunities for participants to get involved in my research, information about presentations that I'm giving, new research findings and new publications. I will also occasionally write bespoke pieces for the blog addressing issues related to my research. On occasion these kinds of pieces have sparked new research projects and have often led to new learning. I am also active on LinkedIn and Twitter/X and have created a YouTube channel, but all of these different accounts feed into and direct people towards the blog.

In addition to my engagement with social media sites, I have also been an enthusiastic user of my university's institutional repository and have used this to make my research openly available through a mixture of self/institutional publishing, publishing in openaccess journals where possible and using both green and gold routes to open access.

I probably use social media every day, and add a blog post about once a week, but I relatively rarely create new content specifically for my online presence. I usually use content that I am creating for other reasons (teaching, presentations and publications) and reuse and adapt this. My decision to take a very open and online approach to research communication has helped me to build an extensive network of people who are potential participants, collaborators and advocates for my research.

Tristram online

Blog	https://adventuresincareerdevelopment.wordpress.com/
LinkedIn	https://www.linkedin.com/in/tristramhooley/
Twitter/X	https://twitter.com/pigironjoe
YouTube	https://www.youtube.com/@pigironjoe
Repository	https://repository.derby.ac.uk/researcher/809wq/tristram-hooley

Rachel Buchanan: For me having an online presence is a part of my work as a researcher. My online social network is as essential to my work as my offline networks. Initially through Twitter/X and lately LinkedIn, I have become a part of a network of scholars working in similar fields. This allows me to share my work with an audience likely to be interested in it and helps me to keep up to date with the work of my peers.

My institutional website and my blog are the more static elements of my online presence, and these present a record of my publications and research projects. I regularly use Twitter/X and LinkedIn for research communication and building and connecting with my online professional network.

As a researcher employed at a public university, I feel that it is important that my research is accessible to the public. Online communication can be a great avenue for knowledge translation. Public blogs such as *The Conversation*, or the blogs of research associations such as BERA and AARE are excellent ways to make research accessible to people outside the academy. I have found that writing about my work on these types of blogs takes my research to a wider audience. Writing for a non-specialist audience has made me a better research communicator.

I use my institutional repository and researcher networking sites such as Academia.edu and ResearchGate to store and share publicly accessible versions of my publications. This strategy means that research is accessible to scholars whose institutions may not have access to paywalled journals.

Like Tristram, I have found that using social media for research communication has helped me to build an online network. Through this network I have developed research collaborations, found research participants and been a lot less lonely as an online researcher than I otherwise would have been.

Rachel online

Profile	https://www.newcastle.edu.au/profile/rachel-buchanan
Blog	https://drbuchananresearch.com/
LinkedIn	https://www.linkedin.com/in/rachel-buchanan-6b51441b3/
Twitter/X	https://twitter.com/rayedish
Academia.Edu	https://newcastle-au.academia.edu/RachelBuchanan

Key issues raised

Our experience of using a range of online tools and platforms to communicate our research has been largely positive, but as the case studies above demonstrate, we have also used this kind of communication for a variety of purposes, ranging from recruitment of participants to research studies, to discussion with peers, to communication of research findings. Given this, it is important to think through what it is that you are hoping to achieve through the online communication of your research and to use this to inform the strategies that you adopt and the tools and platforms that you engage with.

Our case studies also show that it can be difficult to pick one tool. We are active on Twitter, LinkedIn, blogs and academic social media, among other platforms. Each of these takes some time to engage with, so it is important to think carefully about what each new tool offers and whether it is really worth engaging with. Having said that, it can be difficult to understand the benefits of online communication tools until you have tried them. So, it can be a good strategy to experiment and then evaluate what you have got out of it.

It is also important to recognize that different tools help you to connect with different kinds of audiences. If you want to talk to teachers, you want to look for where that community is congregating, if you want to talk to business leaders, they are probably somewhere else. Thinking about your audience is critical to engaging people in your research on social media.

Advantages and disadvantages of communicating your research online

There are a range of advantages in communicating with people about your research using online technologies rather than face to face, print or other alternatives. These advantages include:

- **Speed of communication and ease of access:** In the past, research communication often involved authoring, printing and sending out special publications. This required the involvement of other people (graphic designers, printers and distribution houses) and attracted a cost. Now researchers can publish something to the web that can be accessed by everyone immediately;

- **Opportunity for dialogue:** Most online tools enable two-way communication which means that research communication can quickly become a dialogue with participants, potential collaborators and other interested parties;

- **Increased possibilities for collaboration and peer support:**
  Communicating about your research can quickly grow
  into some form of collaboration. Other researchers may
  offer advice, encouragement or criticism, practitioners or
  policymakers may ask questions or report on their perspective;

- **Improve possibility for monitoring readership and impact:**
  The development of online publication and communication
  of research has massively increased the possibility of
  understanding who your audiences are and what they
  are reading (Cooper, 2015). The science of bibliometrics,
  which uses statistical approaches to analyse the readership,
  citation and usage of research can provide huge insights
  to researchers as well as offering possibilities for the
  management of research which some writers have expressed
  concerns about as they can lead to the surveillance and
  discipline of researchers and their output (Pooley, 2022).

While the internet offers a lot of advantages, it also offers a range of
disadvantages for people communicating research. Many of these
are essentially the flip side of many of the advantages and include:

- **The commitment of substantial amounts of time:** Time is
  one of the most precious qualities and so it is a big negative.
  Online communication tools result in the requirement to
  communicate more and in more ways (Jordan & Weller,
  2018). Academics need to invest time not only to engage in
  communication but also to learn how to use these new tools
  (Radford et al., 2020).

- **Challenges of unfamiliar formats:** There is a growing range
  of ways to communicate your research. Once you have
  mastered blogging and Twitter/X, someone advises you to
  create a TikTok account. Each new tool or platform sucks up
  time and raises questions as to whether you are really getting
  a return on your investment.

- **Being open to criticism and misinterpretation:** The
  internet provides a two-way, and often public, channel of
  communication between you, your participants, your peers,
  stakeholders and the general public. This means that if

people do not like or agree with something that you have said or done, they can tell you. This does not have to be a problem, after all debate and feedback are at the heart of the research process, but you do need to think about how you will address such feedback.

- **Context collapse:** Communicating online is far less regulated and boundaried than conventional forms of academic communication (Radford et al., 2020). Information that you communicate might be intended for one audience but may be read by others. So, scholarly debates between you and your peers may be accessed by participants in your next study to find out about who you are. Managing this context collapse requires careful thought.

- **The possibility of participant-to-participant communication:** It is not only you who has the power of communication. Your participants can also communicate with you and potentially with each other. Depending on the type of research that you are doing, this can be a problem as they may pass on details about your research design that you do not want revealed in advance.

The use of a range of online communication and digital scholarship tools has grown rapidly with some estimates suggesting that more than three quarters of researchers are using at least some digital tools to communicate their research (Sugimoto et al., 2017). While most researchers have viewed such communications as secondary to more traditional forms of academic communication, a minority believe that the use of informal, online approaches to research communication should become increasingly central to research practice (Ellis et al., 2017).

What is different about communicating research online?

Researchers have always communicated with others about their research. In many cases, the use of online forms of communication facilitates existing forms of communication, speeding it up and making it more efficient, but it also alters the paradigm opening new types of communications (Kjelberg et al., 2016). At its most radical, this raises questions as to why we present research in the way that we do. The internet opens up a wide range of new genres for the presentation of research including blogs, film, infographics and interactive web exhibitions. While academic recognition and promotion criteria are likely to keep us connected to books and journal papers for a while; yet there are now many more ways to present data and communicate findings. These new approaches offer greater opportunities for researchers to use image, video material, present greater amounts of participant data and allow readers to have a greater opportunity to explore the findings. Considering how to make use of the greater potential that online presentation of research offers, clearly also poses researchers with new challenges in navigating new genres and deciding where effort is best placed.

One of the most important ways in which it shifts the paradigm is in the creation of a many-to-many communication environment which has the effect of levelling power relations and access to communication tools. In the past a researcher had the potential to write a summary of their research and publish it, but project stakeholders had little opportunity to respond. Now you are typically engaged in a big conversation in which others will often feel empowered to talk back to you.

Some researchers argue that these changes lead to a broader paradigm shift in research. Weller (2011) calls this 'digital scholarship' and notes that the affordances of the online environment can radically change the way in which researchers work. Such changes have implications beyond the communication of research and potentially apply to all aspects of researcher practice (Herman & Nicholas, 2019) and have been identified by researchers as the biggest change that the digital world is bringing to scholarship (Jordan & Weller, 2018).

Building a profile

Successfully communicating research online requires the building of a profile. People need to know who they are communicating with and have some way of contacting you. At its most basic, this can be the inclusion of information about yourself on the university website and the provision of basic contact information such as your email or telephone number. But many researchers now utilize online tools to build a more developed personal profile through which they can communicate with others using blogging platforms, social networking sites or other online tools (Radford et al., 2020).

Building an online profile allows you to communicate with others about *your research*, but it also communicates something about *yourself* to others (Jordan & Weller, 2018). This has led some people to describe the process of building an academic or research profile as being akin to building a brand. For many academics this can be an uncomfortable process for a range of reasons including shyness and a desire for privacy, concern about the commodification of research and engagement with for-profit online social networks which potentially harness the data provided by academics for a range of purposes beyond the control of the researcher (Duffy & Pooley, 2017; Jordan & Weller, 2018; Radford et al., 2020). It also carries with it some reputational risks, as if you say outrageous or inaccurate things, get into online fights or overstep the limits of your expertise; this is all done in public and preserved for posterity.

Some researchers have raised questions as to whether this kind of openness and mobilization of your 'personal brand' is equally available to all researchers, with those researchers working in sensitive and controversial areas, as well as those with certain gender, ethnic or religious identities, more likely to experience discrimination, online harassment and other forms of abuse (Barlow & Awan, 2016). One way that people deal with this is through the adoption of what Pitcan et al. (2018) refer to as a 'vanilla self', that is downplaying non-normative elements of their identity through a process of self-censoring, curating a neutral image and segmenting content by platform. This raises profound questions about this process of 'personal branding' as an element of researcher practice and its potential to reinforce existing hierarchies of gender, class, race and sexuality. This is a subject worthy of further research and critical reflection by researchers, especially those from more privileged backgrounds, as they develop their approach to online self-presentation.

The internet also offers you the opportunity to gather information about yourself and your work that previously would have been difficult to measure (Radford et al., 2020). So, for example, it is possible to find out how many people are viewing your profile, reading your papers, citing them and sharing them with others. This can cut across the conventional ways in which academic performance is measured, with some researchers becoming well-known much earlier in their career through effective online communication, while others with extensive lists of scholarly publications but no online presence languish in obscurity.

The range of forms of academic communication has been expanded in ways that can challenge the ordered and hierarchical way in which the research world has traditionally worked through peer-reviewed journals and other forms of scholarly writing. In many cases, a blog post might be a quicker way to communicate research, but who is checking and quality assuring such posts, and how do they interact with other scholarly activities? Increasingly research funders and universities are recognizing the value of academics having an online profile. Some may even recognize this formally in funding or promotion criteria, so you are not just expected to do good research but also to talk about it publicly and build a reputation among your peers and the wider public.

There are a lot of tools that exist to help academics to build a profile. The most basic invites you to insert information about yourself (usually a photo, short biography, list of publications and so on) and create a webpage which presents this information to the world. However, the concept of building an academic profile goes beyond the simple creation of a 'profile page'. Rather profile building is a relational and communicative activity which involves engaging with others and talking about yourself. Radford et al. (2020) found that researchers who were engaged in profile building connected with other researchers, actively disseminated their academic activities such as the publication of papers and exchanged materials with other researchers. Many concluded that this kind of activity had developed their careers.

Building a network

One way to think about the communication of research is that you are trying to build a network of stakeholders around your research. Such a network may be small or large, comprised mainly of academics or much broader, and it can be largely focused on what you have to say (broadcast) or much more reciprocal.

Since the development of the internet, and particularly since the development of what was at one point called 'Web 2.0', we have had a range of social media platforms which are designed to facilitate the creation and maintenance of social and professional networks.

Many academics and researchers have adopted the use of more mainstream social networks (Facebook, Twitter/X, LinkedIn, etc.) to communicate their research (Kjelberg et al., 2016). It is also worth noting the development of a range of bespoke academic social network sites which have provided platforms for more specialized kinds of academic network (Yan et al., 2021). Although some research has found that the intensity of use of these specialist academic social networks is often low and their impact can be limited (Meishar-Tal & Pieterse, 2017; Muscanell & Utz, 2017). In addition, it is important to recognize the use of a wide range of tools (e.g. blogs, bookmarking tools, citation sharing and management tools) which would not normally be thought of as 'social networking' tools but which include social elements and potentially support the building of networks.

Bespoke academic social networks

Academia.edu (https://www.academia.edu/)
Mendeley (https://www.mendeley.com/)
Researchgate (https://www.researchgate.net/)

The way that researchers build and maintain networks and use social media platforms varies by country, institution and discipline (Kjellberg et al., 2016; Yan et al., 2021). Given this, it is important for researchers to spend time identifying possible tools that could be used to build a network and assessing them both in terms of their functionality, but more importantly in terms of who is active on these sites. The next step is to engage with the site while paying careful attention to the culture and more of the network or community that you are moving into.

The creation of academic networks can lead to conventional types of research collaboration (e.g. joint research projects, publication and conference presentations), but online networks also facilitate a range of more ephemeral types of peer support. For example, many researchers use a range of online tools to ask questions to their network. Questions that are more likely to get an answer tend to be as follows:

- **Short** (at least in the initial ask): Short initial questions which can be easily parsed by readers tend to attract more interest (Deng et al., 2019). Once researchers are engaged then they are typically willing to read longer questions; and

- **From people with a pre-existing reputation**: Researchers are more likely to answer questions posed by people who they have heard of and who they have transacted with in the past.

Open social science

As we have already discussed, the use of the internet has shifted the paradigm of research publication by expanding the types of output that people are producing, enabling outreach to new audiences and creating a movement that argues that the results of research (particularly publicly funded research) should be openly available to everyone (open access).

The open access movement has long roots. There is a strong moral and political case that the public should be able to access the research that they have funded. However, the small-scale, specialist nature of academic journal publishing made this difficult until the birth of the internet and the gradual migration of journal publication online. From the 2000s there started to be an identifiable open access movement calling for research to be made more widely available. By the late 2000s this started to appear in grant funding agreements and to be incentivized in various ways in research measurement and assessment processes (Piwowar et al., 2018).

Over the last twenty years open access has therefore moved from being a somewhat idealistic (but ultimately successful) social movement to being a part of the mainstream of the research environment with approximately a third of all published research articles now available open access (Piwowar et al., 2018). Researchers now often find that they are compelled to make their research available as part of the conditions of funding or as a key requirement of their employment. There is also evidence, albeit with somewhat mixed findings, that open access publishing offers researchers higher levels of citation than research published behind a paywall (Piwowar et al., 2018). Furthermore, many researchers are keen to archive their work for a range of reasons including increasing access to it, increasing their personal brand, altruism and a belief that their decisions to archive will lead to increased sharing (reciprocity) (Lee et al., 2019).

Various definitions of 'open access' exist with the most popular being the Budapest Open Access Initiative's 2002 definition which emphasizes that material should be free to *read and resuse* (Piwowar et al., 2018). While other definitions go for a lighter definition merely requiring that research is free to read. There are a range of different mechanisms that researchers can use to publish their research in an open access form:

- **Self-publishing:** It is possible for researchers to write research notes, papers or even whole books and to self-publish them on their websites or blogs. This is an easy route to open access publishing but lacks any mechanisms for quality assurance and affords little in the way of academic credibility or capital. This sort of approach can also result in work not being indexed in databases and academic search engines.

- **Publishing through repositories:** Most universities now have an institutional research repository. There are also several subject-focused repositories available which provide a publication route for those outside of universities. The criteria for submission to different repositories will vary, but many will allow researchers to deposit working papers and other materials that have not been published elsewhere.

- **Publishing through free open access journals:** There are also a growing number of free (both to publish and to read) open access journals, many of which are run by universities, scholarly societies or other research organizations. These offer a simple open access pathway to publishing.

- **Green route open access publication:** For academics and researchers who are publishing with commercial (non-open) publishers a convention has developed which is often described as the 'green route' option. Green open access is when an author publishes in a journal that is not open access and agrees with the publisher that a copy of the research (usually the author's final, peer-reviewed manuscript) is deposited in either an institutional or subject repository. In this case there is no fee to be paid to the publisher.

- **Gold route open access publication:** Finally, gold open access refers to a published work which is free to access via the publisher's website. This is usually the result of a payment to the publisher by a researcher, their institution or a funder, although other possibilities exist including the possibility for the publisher to open up publications after a period of time or to promote a particular publication theme or to support a particular cause or initiative, for example, during the Covid pandemic some journals, under pressure from governments, were opened up to accelerate the response to the pandemic (UNESCO, 2020).

- **Black route open access publication:** It is difficult for publishers to control what happens to the PDFs and other documents that they create on the internet. Many researchers and other parties freely share published and copyright material online via email, websites and academic social networks. This has led to the growth of a substantial black market where many papers are freely available despite the attempt by publishers to limit access to them to those who have paid. Evidence suggests that use of this black market is rife, even if it may not be legal (Bohannon, 2016).

In addition to the movement to make publications available online there has been a growing push for social researchers to deposit data in data repositories, such as Figshare (https://figshare.com). Depositing data is designed to make research more transparent and to open possibilities for secondary data analysis. Clearly such initiatives require careful thought on the behalf of researchers to ensure appropriate anonymity and address other ethical concerns. Nonetheless, the shift to open data, and the consequent growth in secondary analysis, provides an important direction of travel for social research in the future.

Outreach

Many academics use social media sites such as Twitter/X and blogs to provide them with a channel to present information to a wider audience than would normally be involved in reading academic articles (Singh, 2020). There is also a growing interest in multimedia approaches to communicate research such as podcasts and video sites like YouTube (Sugimoto et al., 2017). As discussed already, the use of such tools raises a range of issues for academics, but particularly when used in parallel with more conventional academic publishing, they can offer powerful tools for communicating with audiences outside of the research community including practitioners in your field or associated fields, students and the wider public.

The shift to engaging with wider audiences has led to the development of the concept of 'alt metrics' (short for *alternative metrics*) which seeks to measure the level of engagement in research beyond conventional academic citations. Alt metrics survey a wide range of social media tools and online environments and summarize the level of engagement with research outputs or researchers in these fora (Sugimoto et al., 2017). The development of 'alt metrics' encourages researchers to move beyond a broadcast mode in which they talk about their research and hope that others are listening, towards a position where they can identify when, where and by who is talking about their work and potentially engage in dialogue.

Career and professional development

The communication of research online can also be viewed as part of the career and professional development of academics. The development of what is sometimes called a *personal learning network*, essentially a bespoke group of people who you can interact with, question and learn from, can be a powerful way for academics to develop their skills and understanding through online interactions (Krutka & Carpenter, 2016).

Academics use technology to facilitate their personal learning environments through the following approaches:

- **Academic back channel**: Social media are used by academics during face-to-face or online events to share information, make social connections and provide commentary on what is being presented (Singh, 2020).

- **Information and resource sharing**: Academics are involved in the routine sharing and consumption of information about research and other topics online. This does not just involve sharing your own research but rather acting as a trusted source of information about and commentary on a range of information sources (Singh, 2020).

- **Social bookmarking and reference management**: The use of online tools such as Zotero (https://www.zotero.org/) to bookmark useful resources and manage references is widespread, with many tools also offering social tools which allow researchers to share their favourite resources and also access the favourites of other researchers.

In addition, the use of digital tools to communicate research can offer researchers benefits in their career such as improved promotion prospects (Chan et al., 2018; Smith & Watson, 2016) and improved well-being (Lupton, 2014), particularly through increased connection to peers (Meishar-Tal & Pieterse, 2017). The development of an individual's profile within research organizations, within the research community and beyond it is perceived to offer career capital, although it can be difficult to provide hard evidence for this (Nicholas et al., 2018). When this is combined with more concrete and well-evident benefits like increased citation rates for open access publication there are at least potential career benefits for academics in taking an active approach to research communication.

The recognition of the benefits of online self-presentation for researchers raises several structural issues, that it is worth considering briefly. First, the kinds of processes that we have described in this chapter are potentially quite labour intensive. If researchers and academics are not only supposed to be engaged in research but also to become bloggers, web designers and marketeers, are their employers going to give them time and resources for these additional tasks? If not, then the desire to communicate online to the public and your peers can quickly become a new form of work intensification, placing researchers under more stress in pursuit of anticipated career rewards. Second, we have briefly touched on the fact that online self-presentation and the presentation of research are more difficult for some researchers than others and that these differences are often organized on existing lines of advantage and disadvantage. Finally, so many of these issues are implicit and intangible, with universities, funders and other research employers often seeking to benefit from the rewards of researchers' online presence while giving little protection and few assurances about how such activities will be valued. Such issues cannot be resolved through the kinds of practice-based hints and tips that we have included in this chapter, nor can they be managed simply by individual withdrawal from the online environment. Rather they require a more collective and structural shift in the way in which researchers work and careers are organized.

In summary

The online communication of research has become an increasingly core part of academic and researcher life. In many ways this has resulted in a paradigm shift in research work. Social researchers can no longer view their audience solely as a narrow technical and expert one. Increasingly research processes and outputs are open for participants and other stakeholders to view.

Some social researchers have viewed this shift as a boon. It is now easier to engage with participants, other researchers, policymakers, practitioners and other stakeholders. Doing so adds purpose and meaning to the process of conducting research and has additional benefits for building your reputation and career. On the other hand, other researchers have emphasized the dark sides of online research communication, highlighting the way that it commodifies research, asks for more (unpaid) labour from researchers, potentially distracts them from their core focus and empowers national and institutional research administrations in surveilling and controlling what researchers do.

Ultimately, we believe that, as with many other aspects of research and academic life, the way in which a researcher engages in research communication and the wider digital world is a question of balance. There is no one-size-fits-all approach to managing research communication or a research career, and so it is important for researchers to think carefully and critically about their own approach and ensure that it aligns with their wider values and research philosophy.

Further reading

There is a wide literature which looks at issues of digital scholarship and at the communication of research online in particular. Mewburn and Clews' (2023) *Be Visible or Vanish: Engage, influence, and Ensure Your Research Has Impact* and Lupton et al.'s (2018) *The Digital Academic* offer a very useful starting point into this literature. More specifically on social media Carrigan's (2019) *Social Media for Academics* and Allen et al.'s (2022) *An Academic's Guide to Social Media* both provides an accessible but thorough guide. For a deeper treatment of the issue see Luzón and Pérez-Llantada's (2022) *Digital Genres in Academic Knowledge Production and Communication.*

CHAPTER NINE

What next for online research methods?

It is always difficult to predict what will happen in the future, and when we are thinking about online research methods, we are trying to make at least three different types of predictions: first, how will technologies develop over the next five to ten or more years; second, how will societies develop, changing the kinds of things that we want to research and how we might go about it; and third, how will research methods including the underpinning philosophies, theories and ethics as well as the regulation and management of research, all change?

This chapter explores current trends in online research and attempts some extrapolation about what the future might hold. It focuses on what the issues are for researchers and considers the strategies that researchers might employ as they navigate the future. But first it is useful to reflect on our past predictions and consider how they have played out.

Looking back, looking forward

In 2012 when we published the first edition of this book, we discussed the likelihood that the growth of online technologies would create a new role for academics and researchers, necessitating the need for new approaches to communication and interaction between researchers and the wider public. This prediction has come to pass to the extent that it is now the basis for a new chapter on online research communications (Chapter 8).

Second, we addressed methodological changes, arguing that the category of 'online research methods' would become less meaningful as most methodological traditions would be online, at least some of the time, by default. The pandemic has played a role in making this prediction come true, but we would argue that the category of online research methods remains valuable as we wrestle with the challenges posed by digital technologies and as a way of supporting cross-disciplinary conversation. In 2012 we observed a trend towards ever more mixing of methods and interdisciplinary and cross-disciplinary work. Although more traditional methodological and disciplinary ways of thinking still have a lot of life left in them, we would continue to emphasize the value of interdisciplinarity as basis for online research methods.

Our third prediction was around the importance of data visualization as an approach. We have addressed this briefly in Chapter 2, but there is more to be said about data visualization methods. There is important work going on in relation to the visualization of administrative data and government open data (Ansari et al., 2022), data gathered online through data mining approaches (Chandra & Dwivedi, 2022) and as a part of social network analysis (Camacho et al., 2020). There has also been the growth of introductory texts explaining how to undertake visualizations (Wilke, 2019) and software to support visualization in qualitative (Andrade et al., 2022) and quantitative research (Blyakhman, 2022; Town & Thabtah, 2019). The use of data visualization is particularly important in relation to big data and associated trends, which we have already discussed in Chapter 2 and elsewhere and which we will return to later in this chapter.

Our next theme from the first edition, was the growth of what we called 'the diverse and integrated internet' which we discuss as 'the internet of things' in Chapter 2 and will return to in this chapter. We anticipated a growing number of devices through which social reality could be experienced and through which social researchers could then gather, observe and produce data. This trend has come to pass and accelerated over the last decade.

We also discussed the growing nature of corporate ownership of data and platforms, what is sometimes referred to as digital enclosure (Grabher, 2020) and argued that this would create challenges for researchers. Again, this process is now much more established and would benefit from further examination from a methodological standpoint. However, in tension with this process of enclosure and corporate control of the internet, we also discussed the potential for the internet to democratize research and 'allow participants to really participate'. This levelling of access to the production of research, the analysis of data and ultimately to a different kind of relationship between experts and the public remains as an important trend in online research methods. We have addressed this in Chapter 8, but it is very much a moving target and important to continue to engage with.

Revisiting predications that are more than a decade old reminds us that continuity is likely to be as important a factor in our predictions of the future as change. The changing role of academics, the increasing embeddedness of digital technologies in the social world, the expanding amount of data alongside our growing ability to organize and analyse it, the tensions between enclosure and democratization, were important themes in the development of online research methods in 2012 and they are, if anything, even more important as we look forward.

While many of the themes remain the same, the way that we conceptualize them has changed following more than a decade of further development in the digital environment and in online research methods. In this chapter we want to discuss these issues under four main headings: first, developments in the datasphere; second, the cataloguing of the world through the IOT; third, the possibilities offered for social research by automation and artificial intelligence; and finally, the growth of theoretical perspectives that can guide the development of online research.

Developments in the datasphere

The concept of the 'datasphere' describes all information, of any type, but importantly including all socially produced information, which can be captured in digital form, as it flows through networks, and is stored, processed and transformed by machines (Bergé et al., 2018). As a society and as a community of social researchers we are still wrestling with the implications of this phenomenon. The fact that such a vast array of human speech, writing, movement and behaviour are representable as data and potentially linkable and analysable, raises fundamental questions about what is possible and desirable to do with such data. Many of these philosophical questions are operationalized at the point at which we begin to engage with the datasphere methodologically.

All online activity, (and, as we will discuss in the next section, increasing amounts of activity in the physical world), produces trace data (Wu & Taneja, 2021). Trace data describes a particular type of metadata made up of the records of user behaviour that are collected by platforms and other apps in logs. Such data is collected and analysed by platform owners to optimize the operations of their own product, manipulate user behaviour in such a way as to increase engagement and maximize profit and to provide a source of income through the selling of data and tailored access to the platform's users (Zuboff, 2019). Indeed, Acker and Donovan (2019) argue that the use of trace data by platforms to manipulate and manage users is an important area worthy of further research. Trace data has the potential to tell researchers a lot about people's interests, behaviours and interactions, but it can be difficult to access and raises questions about ethics, analysis and interpretation. Nonetheless, the consideration of how to use trace data as part of social research is likely to become an increasingly important one over the next few years.

The growth of increasingly corporatized and enclosed digital spaces makes things more difficult for researchers. There is a lot of data, which can tell us a lot about the social world, but much of it is locked behind paywalls, controlled by corporations and is in some cases at the heart of organizations' business models. Some companies may make some data publicly available (e.g. through APIs) in ways that can be used by social researchers, but such data is provided at the whim of the company, and access may be removed suddenly and for reasons that are not necessarily transparent (Bruns, 2019).

Some platforms, such as Google and Facebook, have successfully enclosed not only their own trace data but also trace data about users' engagement with a wider range of sites and online activities (Wu & Taneja, 2021). Indeed, Andrejevic (2022) suggests that we are experiencing a process of 'enclosure creep' in which platforms, and the corporations that own them, are incentivized to enclose more and more of the world's data in search of efficiency and profit. In such cases data owners are unlikely to be willing to share openly with researchers without expecting something back. In some cases what they expect back will be simple and take the form of a financial exchange where data is purchased (Zhu et al., 2019). But, in other cases the payback will be more subtle, often involving the co-option of academic labour into the development of platforms, and the adoption of the standpoint of the platform where the research that is conducted. The political economy of data ownership is largely why attempts to develop industry-academic partnerships to regulate and negotiate data and research sharing have faltered (Wu & Taneja, 2021). The corporations usually have the upper hand in these relationships and researchers often find that they either must compromise their level of access or control to work with such data.

The centrality of platforms to so much of our lives and the way that so much data is produced through interactions with such platforms means that it is easy to view platforms as providing a more complete form of reality than they do. Even Google and Facebook do not know everything about people, not least because people move across a range of different platforms and spend some of their lives away from the glare of digital surveillance. Such a recognition means that social researchers need to develop new approaches to the combination of different online data sources as well as the use of mixed-methods approaches which triangulate, explore and verify the versions of reality that are depicted by platformized big data. Wu and Taneja (2021) note that in previous periods where new forms of data have developed these have fostered new methodological and analytical approaches, and we can anticipate that the same thing will happen going forward. For example, Andreotta et al. (2019) propose a mixed-methodology which uses computational data science to gather and narrow a social media corpus to create a carefully constructed data sub-set that is analysable through qualitative analysis techniques. As we go forward, we can expect more discussions about both computer-supported analytical techniques and about different methodological combinations. But, once again researchers will have to wrestle with ethical issues as they consider whether their findings can and should be incorporated into platforms' algorithms and used to generate more complete forms of surveillance.

There has also been substantial growth in access to public data. Policymakers often lack the capacity to analyse data and so have opened public data such as administrative records to the public, sometimes with additional access available for researchers under special conditions often relating to ethical use and appropriate data protection and control (Penner & Dodge, 2019). Such government-produced and collected big data is unlikely to require the same kind of devil's bargain that researchers may face when accessing data from corporately owned platforms, but it still requires ethical care and methodological rigour. Government data is no more neutral than corporate data and so researchers should be aware of the circumstances and purposes of its collection including the policies that it was designed to monitor or support.

Working with administrative data requires skill in data matching and linkage (Penner & Dodge, 2019). In some countries governments have gone a long way in integrating public data sources, in other countries data sets remain siloed with varying potential for linkage. The possibilities of being able to link health, education, criminal justice and economic data (such as tax records) are enormous, but this is often more difficult in practice than in theory and researchers need to remember that what people tell the government is unlikely to be the full story of their experience. Again, the possibilities for wider data linkages connecting administrative data with corporate trace data and with newly collected research data are exciting but also pose ethical, practical and analytical challenges.

Ultimately many of the considerations around using big data in research revolve around questions of data ownership. This is ultimately a political discussion about who has the right to control data and engage in surveillance. Before the internet, individuals had much greater control by default over their privacy and the right to surveillance was accorded, in limited and specific cases, to the state. The shift to surveillance capitalism (Zuboff, 2019) has radically, but often invisibly, changed this and it seems likely that there will be further legal and political wrangles about where the appropriate boundaries lie. Bruns (2019) argues that researchers should be active participants (what he describes as 'data activists') in these discussions. He goes on to say that there may even be occasions when it is appropriate for researchers to 'break the rules' to do important research in an era of data enclosure, for example using web scraping approaches to access data that is effectively enclosed. This 'anarchic' and activist approach is contested by Puschmann

(2019) who argues that academics should focus on building partnerships with industry to negotiate access.

The enclosed and contested nature of data access means that it is likely to become increasingly politicized in the future. One consequence of this is that questions of consent are likely to become more complex and move beyond simply asking participants for their permission to access and analyse their data, not least because in many cases they may not control this data anyway. Wrangling with such issues is likely to leave researchers managing ethical tension and compromise in their work. In such cases it becomes important to surface issues of data ownership, compromise and the potential dangers of data enclosure in methodological discussions.

Cataloguing the world (the Internet of Things)

We have already introduced the IOT in Chapter 2 and discussed some of its implications throughout the rest of the chapters. Despite this, we would argue that the ability to embed the digital world within the physical world, and vice versa, is going to be one of the most fundamental trends that will shape social research methods into the future. Whether it is tracking research participants' movements and behaviours (Edney et al., 2022), linking consumption patterns to demographics and other data sources (Keikhosrokiani, 2022) or even using 'affective' wearables to monitor emotions, mental health or stress (Kang & Chai, 2022), the integration of the social and physical worlds into the datasphere is rapidly becoming more extensive, with substantial implications for research methods.

These developments are interesting as they transform phenomena that were previously only accessible second hand into data that can be accessed and analysed by researchers. For example, Ng and Wakenshaw (2017) discuss the implications of the IOT for marketing and consumer research. Whereas in the past such research has relied on inference about behaviour from purchasing data, or from self-reported data about usage, researchers will now have 'information and visibility of consumers' actual behaviours and consumption routines (buying, consuming, storing, disposing)' (p. 8). They go on to describe how the use of sensors and wearables could allow research to enter new spaces, such as bathrooms and bedrooms and make experiences like eating a meal, waiting for a bus or buying a new product measurable and relatable to other data such as an individual's health or the weather.

For social researchers such technical possibilities can place behaviours in much richer contexts. We can understand what people are doing, where they are when they are doing it, measure at least some of the influences on them and even gain some insights into how they feel. Of course, such possibilities are reliant on being able to access a wide range of data, which may often be enclosed. Negotiating access is unlikely to be straightforward. Furthermore, the possibility of near-complete surveillance of participants' lives also raises ethical issues about the gaining and managing of consent in a world in which many people are not aware of the level of tracking and dataveillance that they are subject to (Ogunniye & Kokciyan, 2023; Lupton & Williamson, 2017).

Broadly there are two main approaches to using the IOT for social research. In the first researchers make use of naturally occurring data which is already being gathered through the IOT to provide insights into research questions. This might be about finding ways to access things like health, geolocation or consumer data that is generated through people's day-to-day life and tracked through phones or other devices. Such data can be accessed in a variety of ways including gaining access through the organization that owns the app or the data, for example , asking a company to provide access to data about the temperature of its office, footage from its security cameras or employee log on times (Müller et al., 2019). Alternatively, data can be gathered by having participants provide researchers with access to their social media account or feeds or by asking participants to self-report data, for example, the daily number of steps measured by their app (Sun & Jiang, 2022). Accessing such naturally occurring data produced through the IOT can offer researchers a wide range of data including text, multimedia, geolocation data and biometric data. This data can then be related to other data, including both other naturally occurring data and new data collected through surveys, experimental or qualitative methods (Struminskaya et al., 2020).

The second approach is using apps to gather new data as part of a research project. For example, this might be about asking someone to wear a device throughout their time involved in a study or using augmented reality devices to provide information and instructions to participants in experiments or other kinds of social research. Such bespoke approaches are likely to be more expensive and complex than leveraging existing trace data, but they also offer researchers a greater amount of control and may reduce reliance on the corporate owners of existing data (Wu & Taneja, 2021).

Automating research

The growth and increasing ease of access to automation and AI raises possibilities for social researchers but has also led to a justifiable concern about the nature and extent of this automation and what is lost as automation happens. As we were writing this book there was considerable discussion and moral panic around the encroachment of ChatGPT into the production of academic research, much of which was probably unjustified and unhelpful (Lucey & Dowling, 2023).

From a research perspective the emergence of a range of non-human and semi-automated actors such as bots and troll farms raises important questions as to whether the behaviour of such actors should be investigated alongside other research subjects or excluded from analysis. Other researchers have discussed the emergence of an 'AI divide' 'between those who control and manage automated systems and those who are subjected to their machinations' (Andrejevic, 2022, p. 394). Such developments compound and exacerbate many of the ethical and political dilemmas that we have already identified in this book and once again place researchers in challenging positions as they negotiate the intersection of technology, the economy and methodology.

With respect to the production of social research we want to highlight three areas in which automation might be important and helpful. First, the provision of automated support for participants, second the issues of automated data collection and third the issue of automated data analysis.

Throughout this book we have highlighted the importance of a range of ethical considerations including those related to participant consent and data ownership. Ogunniye and Kokciyan (2023) argue that in a world where issues of data ownership and control are becoming both ubiquitous and more complex, it is unrealistic to expect users to meaningfully engage with such questions every time they visit a website or an online research site. An alternative is to provide users with automated privacy assistants to help them to make decisions about what to participate in and how to configure any data agreements that they are allowed to shape (Ogunniye and Kokciyan, 2023). In essence this is about moving away from contractual approaches to privacy and consent in research (where participants are constructed as amateur lawyers and expected to read detailed documents setting out their rights), towards a process whereby automated privacy assistant allow individuals to set out some basic parameters for the management of their data and then allow the assistant to engage with the detail. Such an approach could go beyond following legalistic rules and could give participants an indication of the trustworthiness of the process that they are engaging in, for example by analysing the reputation of the researchers involved. Of course, such approaches require a range of subjective decisions to be made in the design and implementation stage, but at least in principle such approaches offer research participants more support.

It is possible to imagine other ways in which the embedding of automated helpers within research projects could improve the experience of participants. For example, chat bots could be used to answer participants' questions about the research, to help participants to complete complex surveys or experiments, to support participants' understanding of the findings or to provide help, advice and signposting for participants who have found that engaging in the research has raised issues that they want to talk about further.

Second, it is possible to consider a range of ways in which AI might automate the collection of social data. There are a host of ways in which this could happen, including the following possibilities:

- **Automated interviews:** There are a range of well-established AI applications designed to conduct dynamic personal interviews with human subjects. While these have not yet been used much for social research, there is some evidence to support the idea that they may foster disclosure from participants (Pickard & Roster, 2020), especially in discussions of sensitive topics.

- **Drones:** The use of automated and semi-automated drones could be used as a way of recording human settlements, movements and interactions (Hall & Wahab, 2021).

- **Web scraping:** This uses AI to search the web for data based on parameters identified by researchers and then to gather, organize and potentially analyse this data (Khder, 2021).

Finally, it is possible to use forms of automation to support the analysis of data. AI is good at organizing large quantities of data, finding patterns and summarizing these patterns. However, the processes which are used to support this pattern recognition are often difficult to capture and describe. AI analysis often takes place in a black box and is therefore difficult to understand, articulate and reproduce, leading Capogna (2023) to argue that such approaches undermine some of the fundamental components of the scientific method. Such concerns are unlikely to lead all researchers to abandon the use of AI in analysis, but they clearly call for researchers to be careful and critical in their use of such technologies, to consider their limitations and biases carefully and to be transparent in their methodological choices.

The use of AI and machine learning is relatively well established in relation to the analysis of quantitative data where it is often combined with more traditional statistical techniques, particularly in the analysis of large-scale data sets (Di Franco & Santurro, 2021; Grimmer et al., 2021). However, there is growing interest in the use of AI for the analysis of qualitative data (Mockler, 2020b). By using Natural Language Processing (NLP) approaches it is possible to identify themes and code data automatically (Chang et al., 2021). Increasingly such approaches can be used on audio and video material as well as on textual materials. Such approaches also offer the potential to use a mixed-methods paradigm to analyse textual and multimedia data as they typically produce both qualitative summaries (e.g. lists of themes and summaries of different perspectives) as well as quantitative summaries (e.g. quantification of the frequency of how often things are mentioned and how many people are highlighting a particular theme). As the power of NLP increases it may be possible for them to analyse research data alone, but for now it is more typically used to augment qualitative researchers' judgements with the researcher either starting the process of coding and then the machine implementing these patterns (Karamshuk et al., 2017), or the researcher observing the patterns that have been identified, naming them and considering their significance. Automated qualitative analysis may also make use of sentiment analysis tools to allow for the summary of affective trends and patterns in qualitative data, including large data sets (Birjali et al., 2021).

When combined with machine translation, the use of NLP also increases the possibilities for cross-cultural and multi-language studies. The ability to interrogate data produced in other linguistic settings, either through translation or through NLP approaches, offers social researchers' possibilities for entirely new types of comparative study. But studies on machine translation in other contexts would suggest some caution regarding such developments, noting the likelihood of missing subtleties, contextual meaning and potentially heightening existing linguistic inequalities rather than mitigating them (Vieira et al., 2021).

Theoretical perspectives

New theories are wrestling with the way in which the socio-technological innovations described in this chapter are changing the social world. Many such theories are interested in the interaction between the digital and physical worlds. At the heart of these theories are fundamental ontological and epistemological questions which ask what it is to be human and whether human subjects can be meaningfully, helpfully and ethically reduced to data.

Theoretical approaches that allow for nuanced and interdisciplinary exploration of the socio-technological world are likely to grow in prominence in coming years. Such perspectives include posthumanism, new materialism and postdigital theory. Posthumanism challenges the traditional anthropocentric view of human beings as the pinnacle of evolution and instead considers the human condition as a process of becoming, in constant interaction with technology and other non-human entities (Braidotti, 2013). While some branches of posthumanist philosophy (transhumanist perspectives in particular) embrace the possibility and consequences of transcending human limitations (physical and cognitive), through technological enhancement and evolution, critical posthumanists see this position as reinscribing the humanist view of humanity's supremacy.

Posthuman theorists question the boundaries between the human and the non-human, challenging the idea that human beings are separate and distinct from the natural world. They argue that human identity is not fixed but rather shaped by complex networks of material and social forces, including technology, language and culture (Braidotti, 2013). Posthuman theory has relevance for social researchers, as it prompts us to rethink our relationship with technology, nature and ourselves. It also raises ethical and political questions about the distribution of power, access to resources and the impact of technological advances on society and the environment (Braidotti, 2021).

Like posthumanism, new materialism is a theoretical and philosophical perspective that emerged as a response to the limitations of traditional human-centred approaches to understanding the world. New materialism challenges traditional views of materiality, agency and subjectivity and emphasizes the active role of non-human entities, such as matter, technology and the environment, in shaping human experience and social relations (Bennett, 2010). Building on the work of Spinoza, and Deleuze and Guattari, new materialists reject the dualistic view of mind and body and instead emphasize the materiality of thought and the embodied nature of perception. New materialism challenges the idea that agency is limited to conscious, intentional human actions. Agency is seen as distributed throughout the world, enacted by a complex network of material and social forces – a helpful theoretical perspective when grappling with the material impacts of non-human actors, such as chat bots, algorithms and AI. New materialism emphasizes the interconnectedness of all entities, human and non-human and the importance of recognizing the agency and vitality of non-human entities in shaping the world around us.

Postdigital theory offers a means of exploring the impact of digital technology on human society and culture, and the ways in which we can move beyond a binary distinction between the 'digital' and the 'real'. It emerged in response to the limitations of the 'digital divide' discourse, which emphasizes access to technology as the primary factor that determines social and economic inequality (Jandrić et al., 2019).

Postdigital theory acknowledges that digital technology has become pervasive and integral to most aspects of our lives, and that it has altered the way we experience and understand reality (Arndt et al., 2019). Proponents of postdigital theory reject the notion that the digital and the non-digital are separate or opposed, instead seeing them as deeply interconnected and co-constitutive. Postdigital theorists emphasize the need to critically engage with digital technology and its effects, rather than simply celebrating or denouncing it. It acknowledges that technology is not neutral, and that it can both enable and constrain our agency and creativity. Postdigital theory represents a more nuanced and reflexive approach to the use of, and research into technology, one that considers the social, ethical, political and cultural implications of our choices. These philosophical perspectives, along with more established theories, such as actor-network theory (Lugosi & Quinton, 2018) offer a means of accounting for and exploring non-human actors in social research.

The growth of these such theories reminds us of the challenges of viewing theory and method separately. The growth of the datasphere, the IOT, automation and AI present us with challenges and questions about what social reality is, and it is important to address these questions alongside the more technical methodological questions about how we find out about social reality. Kar and Dwivedi (2020) caution against the tendency to be overwhelmed by the volume of data and the availability of tools to analyse it and argue that it is vital that researchers use and develop theory to move beyond the 'what' and remain focused on the question of 'why'. They go on to argue that theory building is often supported by rigorous validation of findings, criticality about what data means and how it has been collected and a willingness to use mixed-methods and mixed-mode approaches. A similar point is made by Capogna (2023), coming at these issues from a different disciplinary perspective, who cautions that researchers must not lose their sociological imaginations either through fear of growing complexity or in response to the promises that experience can be datified and easily represented.

Final thoughts

This book has set out the key trends and evidence on online social research methods. In this chapter we have looked forward and surfaced some of the main trends in social research that are likely to shape the future. To conclude it is perhaps useful to consider what the social researcher of the future might be like.

Online research methods are cross-disciplinary, multi-mode and multi-method. Consequently, there will be no one type of online researcher, but whether you are an ethnographer or a quantitative economist, it is impossible not to recognize that digital technologies, data and the digital mediation of experience are becoming increasingly pervasive. While we would urge caution in any absolute predictions about the trajectory of the social world, it seems very unlikely that digital integration is going to go into reverse. This means that as we move forward into the future there are likely to be more social researchers using online and digital methods, and online research methods are going to become increasingly mainstream. We would also argue that a recognition of the value of interdisciplinarity and mixed-methods and multi-mode approaches is likely to be important for some, if not all, of the future generation of online researchers.

Second, we have highlighted the ethical issues involved in online social research in every chapter of this book. In this chapter we have highlighted some of the most difficult and emerging ethical issues. The growth of the internet has not proved to be the great leveller that some predicted, rather it has created new forms of enclosure, hierarchy and inequality. The online researcher is destined to struggle with and manage this imperfect world. Effective online researchers will be defined by their ability to think carefully, critically and in sophisticated and flexible ways about moral, ethical and philosophical issues. The ethical role of researchers may be growing, with a need for researchers to support participants' understanding of these issues and to be able to intervene into socio-technological debates where they impact on research and on the lives of participants.

Third, there is a growing need for researchers with high degrees of digital and technical understanding and literacy. The possibilities discussed in this chapter of working with big data, the IOT and AI are all reliant on researchers' technical ability or their ability to build interdisciplinary collaborations that can support them to undertake more technically complex research.

Finally, it is important that social research remains primarily focused on its main objective, the discovery and analysis of the social world. Online research offers access to a seductive array of data, tools and technologies. But ultimately these are means to an end and that the end is the generation of new theories and insights about how people live their lives, how societies are organized and increasingly about how the intersection of the digital and the physical are shaping social realities.

GLOSSARY

One of the principal challenges in undertaking online research is the need to penetrate the language. This glossary demystifies the technological terminology that the online researcher is required to master. Understanding the wide range of tools, environments and online cultures within which online research is conducted is an essential precursor to undertaking online research.

Affordance An affordance is what a user can do with an object or application. An affordance is not a 'property' of an object, rather it is a result of the relationship between the user and the object.

API (Application Programming Interface) A programming code that connects computer programmes together.

Apps (applications) A software programme that is designed to perform a specific function directly for the user or, in some cases, for another application programme.

Artificial intelligence (AI) A computer programme or a robot controlled by a computer that undertakes tasks that are usually done by humans because they require human intelligence and discernment.

Asynchronous is used to describe communications which are not required to take place at a set time. The data can be transmitted intermittently rather than in a steady stream. For example, an asynchronous online interview will usually involve the interviewer posting to a discussion list or emailing interview questions to respondents to answer at their own convenience. Neither party needs to be online at the same time.

Avatar is the graphical depiction of an individual online. It is commonly applied to characters used in virtual reality or online gaming environments.

Bibliometrics The statistical analyses of books, articles or other publications. This can be used to track author or researcher output and impact or to investigate patterns and themes in publications.

Big data is a description of the exponential increase in the amount of analysable data. This might include both information generated online and information that is made accessible in other ways that can be analysed and related together. Big data is often described as being defined by volume, velocity, variety, veracity (data integrity and authenticity) and value (the financial or research value of the data to the organization or study).

Blogs are websites composed of serial short or medium length entries. Most blogs are interactive, allowing visitors to leave comments and even message each other via widgets on the blogs, and it is this interactivity that distinguishes them from other static websites. Blogs may be maintained by individuals or a collaborating group.

Bot A software programme that performs repetitive tasks especially online. See also *chatbot*

CAQDAS (Computer Assisted Qualitative Data Analysis Software) A range of software applications that aid in the analysis of qualitative data.

Chatbot A computer programme (often using AI) that stimulates conversation with human users online.

Chat room Chat is a facility allowing real-time text-based communication between two or more users in virtual places known as 'chat rooms'. This usually makes use of IRC (Internet Relay Chat) technology.

Cloud (the cloud) describes all of the content and services that can be accessed remotely over the internet. This means that *cloud computing* is the delivery of computing services including servers, storage, databases, networking, software, analytics and intelligence over the internet.

Dark web is the part of the web that is only accessible by means of special software, which allows users and content and service providers to remain anonymous or untraceable.

Data centres A facility that provides shared access to applications and data using a complex network, computing and storage infrastructure.

Data mining The application of techniques, including *machine learning* and *artificial intelligence*, to large data sets or databases to identify patterns.

Deep web The part of the World Wide Web that is not discoverable by means of standard search engines, including password-protected or dynamic pages and encrypted networks.

Digital divide The digital divide is a term that refers to the gap between individuals, demographics and regions that have access to, or competence in, digital technologies.

Digital enclosure A term used to describe the way in which corporations and platforms increasingly own and control people's data. This process is likened to historic processes of the enclosure of common land by landlords.

Doxxing means to search for and publish private or identifying
information about a particular individual or organization on the
internet, typically with malicious intent.

Elicited data Information gathered from participants in response to
researchers' questions or prompts.

Flaming General term for aggressive or insulting messages or posts.
A Flame War is used to describe a situation in which an online
discussion becomes a series of aggressive exchanges or personal
attacks.

Global Positioning System (GPS) is a 'constellation' of twenty-four well-
spaced satellites that orbit Earth and make it possible for people with
ground receivers to pinpoint their geographic location. The location
accuracy is anywhere from 100 to 10 metres for most equipment. GPS
equipment is widely used in science and has now become sufficiently
low-cost so that almost anyone can own a GPS receiver.

Hashtag A hashtag, represented by the hash symbol '#', is a type of
metadata tag used on social media platforms to categorize and make
content discoverable. When a user includes a hashtag in their post,
it becomes a link to other posts that have used the same hashtag.
Hashtags can be used for a wide variety of purposes, such as to join
conversations, express emotions, promote brands or causes or organize
events. They are widely used on platforms like Twitter/X, Instagram,
Facebook and TikTok.

Internet A global public system of interconnected computer networks.

Internet of Things (IOT) The interconnection via the internet of
computing devices embedded in everyday objects, enabling them to
send and receive data.

IP address (also known as 'IP number' or simply 'IP'). This is a code
made up of numbers separated by three dots that identifies a particular
computer on the internet. Every computer, whether it be a web server
or your home computer, requires an IP address to connect to the
internet. IP addresses consist of four sets of numbers from 0 to 255,
separated by three dots.

Internet Relay Chat (IRC) This is a form of real-time (synchronous)
digital communication. IRC is often used by groups on discussion
forums, but this type of 'chat' can also be used on a one-to-one basis to
send private messages.

Last mile refers to the part of the internet that connects the devices in
homes, schools and businesses to the internet. This includes the towers
that allow people to connect to the internet using their mobile phones.

Lists, listserv or email lists A list or listserv is a specialized use of email
in which individuals or groups distribute information to a widespread
group of internet users by using list of email addresses. This works in
the same way that a traditional mailing list might be employed to send

information to a group of subscribers. The listserv itself is owned by a specific software company and is a registered trademark.

Lurking The act of watching others contributing to an online forum, discussion or network without contributing.

Machine learning Artificial intelligence approaches which use software to improve their ability to perform a task, such as the analysis of data, through experience.

Metadata A set of data that describes and gives information about other data.

Micro-blogs A medium which allows users to broadcast short entries (typically 140 characters or less) in the form of a text, a picture, or a brief video clip to other users of the service.

MTurk (Amazon Mechanical Turk) A crowdsourcing marketplace that makes it easier for individuals and businesses to outsource their processes and jobs to a distributed workforce who can perform these tasks virtually. This can include participation in research as well as research tasks such as coding and analysis.

Natural Language Processing (NLP) Techniques which use computational approaches to analyse textual data which is written in 'natural language'.

Naturally occurring data Data that is generated and exists independently of, and without researcher involvement.

Nonprobability sampling is the selection of participants through non-random methods such as convenience sampling, quota sampling or purposive sampling.

Offline The state of not being connected to the internet.

Online The state of being connected to the internet.

Onsite A description of activities which do not require the internet.

Personal learning network (PLE) An individual's network (not necessarily online) that describes the group of people that they connect with to access and contribute ideas, questions, reflections and content.

Platforms A term used to describe a range of services available on the internet including marketplaces, search engines, social media, creative content outlets, app stores, communications services, payment systems and services comprising.

Populations are the total group of people being studied. Researchers will commonly be unable to interact with everyone being studied (the population) and will therefore need to work with a sample.

Probability sampling The selection of a sample from a population, when this selection is based on the principle of randomization, that is, random selection or chance.

Questionnaires are tools or instruments which researchers use to undertake a survey. They usually comprise a series of questions or stimulus for response.

Recruitment is used to describe the ways in which participants are encouraged to take part in the researcher's survey.

Reddit Reddit is a social news website and forum where content is socially curated and promoted by site members through voting.

Response rates describe the number of people who participated in a survey in relation to the number of people in the sample. It is often expressed as a percentage.

Samples are part of a population which is examined for the purpose of drawing inferences about the population as a whole. Quantitative researchers may use statistical techniques to determine their sample and to analyse the data they gather.

Small data Data that is 'small' enough for human comprehension. It is data in a volume and format that makes it accessible, informative and actionable.

Social media Term used to describe a variety of web-based platforms, applications and technologies that enable people to socially interact with one another online. Some examples of social media sites and applications include Facebook, YouTube, Twitter/X, TikTok, Instagram, blogs and other sites that have content based on user participation and user-generated content (UGC).

Surface web The portion of the World Wide Web that is readily available to the general public and searchable with standard web search engines.

Synchronous is used to describe communications which take place in 'real time' in an environment such as an internet chat room. A good example of this is online interviews, where all participants must be online simultaneously and questions and answers are posted in a way which mimics a traditional interview.

Trace data Trace data describes the records of user behaviour that are collected by platforms and other apps in logs.

Troll An actor who uses the internet to deliberately provoke others. A *troll farm* is an institutionalized group of trolls that seeks to interfere in political processes and shape opinions, usually for a political or economic purpose.

Viral content Content that is said to have 'gone viral' has spread rapidly and extensively among a large number of people through online sharing, typically on social media platforms.

Virtual worlds are online communities where users can interrelate with each other and use and create various objects. Typically, virtual worlds take the form of a computer based simulated environment.

Virtual Learning Environment (VLE) A system which is designed to work over the internet to provide support for teaching and learning in educational settings.

Virtual Reality (VR) can be defined as a synthetic or virtual environment which gives a person a sense of reality. This definition would include any synthetic environment which gives a person a feeling of 'being there'. VR generally refers to environments which are computer generated, although there are several immersive environments which are not entirely synthesized by computer.

Web 2.0 A popular buzzword among the technical and marketing communities, used to describe a perceived shift in the use of world wide web technology and web design, which emphasizes the importance of information-sharing, creativity and collaboration among internet users. The term (coined in 2004 by O'Reilly Media) refers to changes in the ways existing internet facilities are used, rather than to an actual 'second generation' of web technology. The increased use of interactive internet-based services such as social networking sites, blogs, video-sharing sites, wikis and forums has led to a movement away from static, read-only webpages towards dynamic websites whose content is shaped partially or entirely by their users.

Web/www/world wide web Part of the internet that contains linked text, image, sound and video documents. Before www, information retrieval on the internet was text-based and required that users know basic UNIX commands. The web has gained popularity largely because of its ease of use (point-and-click graphical interface) and multimedia capabilities, as well as its convenient access to other types of internet services (such as email).

Web scraping A process used to extract data from websites. The term typically refers to automated processes implemented using a bot or web crawler to gather web data into a local database or spreadsheet, for later retrieval or analysis.

REFERENCES

Abrams, K. M., & Gaiser, T. J. (2016). Online focus groups. In N. G. Fielding, R. M. Lee, & G. Blank (Eds.), *The Sage handbook of online research methods* (2nd ed., pp. 435–50). SAGE.

Abrams, K. M., Wang, Z., Song, Y. J., & Galindo-Gonzalez, S. (2015). Data richness trade-offs between face-to-face, online audiovisual, and online text-only focus groups. *Social Science Computer Review*, *33*(1), 80–96. https://doi.org/10.1177/0894439313519733

Acker, A., & Donovan, J. (2019). Data craft: A theory/methods package for critical internet studies. *Information, Communication & Society*, *22*(11), 1590–609. https://doi.org/10.1080/1369118X.2019.1645194

Acocella, I., & Cataldi, S. (2021). *Using focus groups: Theory, methodology, practice*. SAGE. https://dx.doi.org/10.4135/9781529739794

Adams-Hutcheson, G., & Longhurst, R. (2017). 'At least in person there would have been a cup of tea': Interviewing via Skype. *Area*, *49*(2), 148–55. https://doi.org/10.1111/area.12306

Adjerid, I., & Kelley, K. (2018). Big data in psychology: A framework for research advancement. *American Psychologist*, *73*, 899–917. https://doi.org/10.1037/amp0000190

Adler, K., Salanterä, S., & Zumstein-Shaha, M. (2019). Focus group interviews in child, youth, and parent research: An integrative literature review. *International Journal of Qualitative Methods*, *18*, 1609406919887274. https://doi.org/10.1177/1609406919887274

Aghazadeh, S. A., Burns, A., Chu, J., Feigenblatt, H., Laribee, E., Maynard, L., Meyers, A. L. M., O'Brien, J. L., & Rufus, L. (2018). GamerGate: A case study in online harassment. In J. Golbeck (Ed.), *Online harassment* (pp. 179–207). Springer International Publishing.

Allen, K. A., Jimerson, S. R., Quintana, D. S., & McKinley, L. (2022). *An academic's guide to social media: Learn, engage, and belong*. Routledge.

Andrade, C. (2020). The limitations of online surveys. *Indian Journal of Psychological Medicine*, *42*(6), 575–6. https://doi.org/10.1177/0253717620957496

Andrade, L. R. D. S., Linhares, R. N., Costa, A. P., & Souza, F. S. D. C. (2022). Data visualisation in software supporting qualitative analysis. *Acta Scientiarum. Education*, 44. https://doi.org/10.4025/actascieduc .v44i1.52857

Andrejevic, M. (2022). Meta-Surveillance in the digital enclosure. *Surveillance & Society*, 20(4), 390–6. https://doi.org/10.24908/ss.v20i4 .16008

Andreotta, M., Nugroho, R., Hurlstone, M. J., Boschetti, F., Farrell, S., Walker, I., & Paris, C. (2019). Analyzing social media data: A mixed-methods framework combining computational and qualitative text analysis. *Behavior Research Methods*, 51, 1766–81. https://doi.org/10 .3758/s13428-019-01202-8

Angelone, L. (2019). Virtual ethnography: The post possibilities of not being there. *Mid-Western Educational Researcher*, 31(3), 275–95.

Ansari, B., Barati, M., & Martin, E. G. (2022). Enhancing the usability and usefulness of open government data: A comprehensive review of the state of open government data visualization research. *Government Information Quarterly*, 39(1), 101657. https://doi.org/10.1016/j.giq .2021.101657

Ansolabehere, S., & Schaffner, B. F. (2014). Does survey mode still matter? Findings from a 2010 multi-mode comparison. *Political Analysis*, 22(3), 285–303. https://doi.org/10.1093/pan/mpt025

Antoun, C., Couper, M. P., & Conrad, F. G. (2017). Effects of mobile versus PC web on survey response quality: A crossover experiment in a probability web panel. *Public Opinion Quarterly*, 81(S1), 280–306. https://doi.org/10.1093/poq/nfw088

Archer, C. (2019). Social media influencers, post-feminism and neoliberalism: How mum bloggers' 'playbour' is reshaping public relations. *Public Relations Inquiry*, 8(2), 149–66. https://doi.org/10. 1177/2046147X19846530

Archibald, M. M., Ambagtsheer, R. C., Casey, M. G., & Lawless, M. (2019). Using Zoom videoconferencing for qualitative data collection: Perceptions and experiences of researchers and participants. *International Journal of Qualitative Methods*, 18, 160940691987459. https://doi.org/10.1177/1609406919874596

Arechar, A. A., Gächter, S., & Molleman, L. (2018). Conducting interactive experiments online. *Experimental Economics*, 21(1), 99–131. https://doi.org/10.1007/s10683-017-9527-2

Arndt, S., Asher, G., Knox, J., Ford, D. R., Hayes, S., Lăzăroiu, G., Jackson, L., Contreras, J. M., Buchanan, R., D'Olimpio, L., Smith, M., Suoranta, J., Pyyhtinen, O., Ryberg, T., Davidsen, J., Steketee, A., Mihăilă, R., Stewart, G., Dawson, M., & Peters, M. A. (2019). Between the blabbering noise of individuals or the silent dialogue of many: A collective response to 'Postdigital Science and Education' (Jandrić et al. 2018). *Postdigital Science and Education.* https://doi.org/10.1007/s42438-019-00037-y

Atkinson, P. (2022). *Crafting ethnography.* SAGE.

Attewell, P., Monaghan, D., & Kwong, D. (2015). *Data mining for the social sciences: An introduction.* University of California Press.

Au, C. H., Ho, K. K., & Chiu, D. K. (2021). Does political extremity harm the ability to identify online information validity? Testing the impact of polarisation through online experiments. *Government Information Quarterly, 38*(4), 101602. https://doi.org/10.1016/j.giq.2021.101602

Auer, M., & Griffiths, M. D. (2022). Gambling before and during the COVID-19 pandemic among online casino gamblers: An empirical study using behavioral tracking data. *International Journal of Mental Health and Addiction, 20*(3), 1722–32. https://doi.org/10.1007/s11469 -020-00462-2

August, T., Oliveira, N., Tan, C., Smith, N., & Reinecke, K. (2018). Framing effects: Choice of slogans used to advertise online experiments can boost recruitment and lead to sample biases. *Proceedings of the ACM on Human-Computer Interaction, 2*(CSCW), 1–19. https://doi .org/10.1145/3274291

Ball, H. L. (2019). Conducting online surveys. *Journal of Human Lactation, 35*(3), 413–17. https://doi.org/10.1177/0890334419848734

Barlow, C., & Awan, I. (2016). 'You need to be sorted out with a knife': The attempted online silencing of women and people of Muslim faith within academia. *Social Media+ Society, 2*(4), 2056305116678896. https://doi.org/10.1177/2056305116678896

Barnes, N. (2021). The social life of literacy education: How the 2018 #phonicsdebate is reshaping the field. *The Australian Educational Researcher, 49*(2), 243–60. https://doi.org/10.1007/s13384-021 -00451-x

Barnes, N., Watson, S., & MacRae, S. (2022). The moral positioning of education policy publics: How social media is used to wedge an issue. *Critical Studies in Education,* https://doi.org/10.1080/17508487.2022 .2153372

Barnhoorn, J. S., Haasnoot, E., Bocanegra, B. R., & van Steenbergen, H. (2015). QRTEngine: An easy solution for running online reaction time experiments using Qualtrics. *Behavior Research Methods, 47*(4), 918–29. https://doi.org/10.3758/s13428-014-0530-7

Barrow, J. M., Brannan, G. D., & Khandhar, P. B. (2022). *Research ethics.* StatPearls Publishing.

Batrinca, B., & Treleaven, P. C. (2015). Social media analytics: A survey of techniques, tools and platforms. *AI & Society, 30*, 89–116. https://doi .org/10.1007/s00146-014-0549-4

Beaudouin, V., & Velkovska, J. (1999). The Cyberians: An empirical study of sociality in a virtual community. In K. Buckner (Ed.), *Proceedings of Esprit i3 Workshop on Ethnographic Studies in Real and Virtual Environments: Inhabited Information Spaces and Connected Communities* (pp. 102–12). Inhabited Information Spaces and Connected Communities.

Bednarek, M., & Carr, G. (2021). Computer-assisted digital text analysis for journalism and communications research: Introducing corpus linguistic techniques that do not require programming. *Media International Australia*, *181*(1), 131–51. https://doi.org/10.1177/1329878X20947124

Beer, D. (2017). The social power of algorithms. *Information, Communication & Society*, *20*(1). 1–13. https://doi.org/10.1080/1369118X.2016.1216147

Benbunan-Fich, R. (2017). The ethics of online research with unsuspecting users: From A/B testing to C/D experimentation. *Research Ethics*, *13*(3–4), 200–18. https://doi.org/10.1177/1747016116680664

Bennett, J. (2010). A vitalist stopover on the way to a new materialism. In D. Cole & S. Frost (Eds.), *New materialisms: Ontology, agency, and politics* (pp. 47–69). Duke University Press.

Bergé, J. S., Grumbach, S., & Zeno-Zencovich, V. (2018). The 'datasphere', data flows beyond control, and the challenges for law and governance. *European Journal of Comparative Law and Governance*, *5*(2), 144–78. https://doi.org/10.1163/22134514-00502001

Bernal, P. (2020). *What do we know and what should we do about internet privacy?* SAGE.

Biffignandi, S., & Bethlehem, J. (2021). *Handbook of web surveys*. Wiley.

Birjali, M., Kasri, M., & Beni-Hssane, A. (2021). A comprehensive survey on sentiment analysis: Approaches, challenges and trends. *Knowledge-Based Systems*, *226*, 107134. https://doi.org/10.1016/j.knosys.2021.107134

Birnbaum, M. H. (2009). Designing online experiments. In A. Joinson, K. Y. A. McKenna, T. Postmes & U-D. Reips (Eds.), *Oxford Handbook of Internet Psychology*. (pp. 391–404). Oxford University Press.

Blair, E., & Blair, J. (2014). *Applied survey sampling*. SAGE.

Blyakhman, A. (2022). Selecting data visualization tools. *Strategic Finance*, *103*(12), 62–3.

Boellstorff, T. (2012). Rethinking digital anthropology. In H. A. Horst & D. Miller (Eds.), *Digital anthropology*. Routledge.

Bohannon, J. (2016). Who's downloading pirated papers? Everyone. *Science*, *325*, 6285. https://www.science.org/doi/full/10.1126/science.352.6285.508

Bond, R. M., Fariss, C. J., Jones, J. J., Kramer, A. D., Marlow, C., Settle, J. E., & Fowler, J. H. (2012). A 61-million-person experiment in social influence and political mobilization. *Nature*, 489(7415), 295–8. https://doi.org/10.1038/nature11421

Bosnjak, M., Das, M., & Lynn, P. (2016). Methods for probability-based online and mixed-mode panels: Selected recent trends and future perspectives. *Social Science Computer Review*, 34(1), 3–7. https://doi.org/10.1177/0894439315579246

boyd, d., & Crawford, K. (2012). Critical questions for big data: Provocations for a cultural, technological, and scholarly phenomenon. *Information, Communication & Society*, 15(5), 662–79. https://doi.org/10.1080/1369118X.2012.678878

Braidotti, R. (2013). *The posthuman*. Polity Press.

Braidotti, R. (2021). *Posthuman feminism*. Wiley.

Brinkmann, S., & Kvale, S. (2014). *InterViews: Learning the craft of qualitative research interviewing* (3rd ed.). SAGE.

Brooker, P. (2022). Computational ethnography: A view from sociology. *Big Data & Society*, 9(1), 20539517211069892. https://doi.org/10.1177/20539517211069892

Bruns, A. (2019). After the 'APIcalypse': Social media platforms and their fight against critical scholarly research. *Information, Communication & Society*, 22(11), 1544–66. https://doi.org/10.1080/1369118X.2019.1637447

Bucci, M., & Trench, B. (Eds.). (2021). *Routledge handbook of public communication of science and technology*. Routledge.

Buchanan, E. A., & Zimmer, M. (2021). Internet research ethics. In E. N. Zalta (Ed.), *The Stanford encyclopedia of philosophy*. Metaphysics Research Lab, Stanford University.

Burger, N., Charness, G., & Lynham, J. (2011). Field and online experiments on self-control. *Journal of Economic Behavior & Organization*, 77(3), 393–404. https://doi.org/10.1016/j.jebo.2010.11.010

Bytzek, E., & Bieber, I. E. (2016). Does survey mode matter for studying electoral behaviour? Evidence from the 2009 German Longitudinal Election Study. *Electoral Studies*, 43, 41–51. https://doi.org/10.1016/j.electstud.2016.04.007

Cabiria, J. (2015). Interviewing in virtual worlds: An application of best practices. In J. Salmons (Ed.), *Cases in Online Interview Research* (pp. 109–30). SAGE. https://doi.org/10.4135/9781506335155.n4

Callegaro, M., Manfreda, K. L., & Vehovar, V. (2014). *Web survey methodology*. SAGE.

Camacho, D., Panizo-LLedot, Á., Bello-Orgaz, G., Gonzalez-Pardo, A., & Cambria, E. (2020). The four dimensions of social network analysis: An overview of research methods, applications, and software tools.

Information Fusion, 63, 88–120. https://doi.org/10.1016/j.inffus.2020
.05.009

Capogna, S. (2023). Sociology between big data and research frontiers,
a challenge for educational policies and skills. *Quality & Quantity*,
1–20. https://doi.org/10.1007/s11135-022-01351-7

Carrigan, M. (2019). *Social media for academics*. SAGE.

Chan, T. M., Stukus, D., Leppink, J., Duque, L., Bigham, B. L., Mehta, N.,
& Thoma, B. (2018). Social media and the 21st-century scholar: How
you can harness social media to amplify your career. *Journal of the
American College of Radiology, 15*(1), 142–8. https://doi.org/10.1016
/j.jacr.2017.09.025

Chandler, J., Mueller, P., & Paolacci, G. (2014). Nonnaïveté among
Amazon Mechanical Turk workers: Consequences and solutions for
behavioral researchers. *Behavior Research Methods, 46*(1), 112–30.
https://doi.org/10.3758/s13428-013-0365-7

Chandler, J., Paolacci, G., Peer, E., Mueller, P., & Ratliff, K. A. (2015).
Using nonnaive participants can reduce effect sizes. *Psychological
Science, 26*(7), 1131–9. https://doi.org/10.1177/0956797615585115

Chandra, T. B., & Dwivedi, A. K. (2022). Data visualization: Existing
tools and techniques. In S. De, S. Dey, S. Bhattacharyya, & S. Bhatia.
(Eds.), *Advanced data mining tools and methods for social computing*
(pp. 177–217). Academic Press.

Chang, T., DeJonckheere, M., Vydiswaran, V. V., Li, J., Buis, L. R., &
Guetterman, T. C. (2021). Accelerating mixed methods research with
natural language processing of big text data. *Journal of Mixed Methods
Research, 15*(3), 398–412. https://doi.org/10.1177/15586898211021196

Chang, T. Z. D., & Vowles, N. (2013). Strategies for improving data
reliability for online surveys: A case study. *International Journal of
Electronic Commerce Studies, 4*(1), 121–30. https://doi.org/10.7903/
ijecs.1121

Charlesworth, A. (2015). Data protection and research data. https://www
.jisc.ac.uk/full-guide/data-protection-and-research-data

Chaudhuri, A. (2021). *Behavioural economics and experiments*. Routledge.

Chen, Y., & Konstan, J. (2015). Online field experiments: A selective
survey of methods. *Journal of the Economic Science Association, 1*(1),
29–42. https://doi.org/10.1007/s40881-015-0005-3

Chiluwa, I. E., & Samoilenko, S. A. (2019). *Handbook of research on
deception, fake news, and misinformation online*. Information Science
Reference/IGI Global.

Chopra, K., Gupta, K., & Lambora, A. (2019). Future internet: The internet
of things-A literature review. *2019 International Conference on Machine
Learning, Big Data, Cloud and Parallel Computing (COMITCon)*,
135–9. https://doi.org/10.1109/COMITCon.2019.8862269

Christin, A. (2020). The ethnographer and the algorithm: Beyond the black box. *Theory and Society, 49*(5), 897–918. https://doi.org/10 .1007/s11186-020-09411-3

Chua, S. M. (2022). Navigating conflict between research ethics and online platform terms and conditions: A reflective account. *Research Ethics, 18*(1), 39–50. https://doi.org/10.1177/17470161211045526

Coleman, R. (2018). *Designing experiments for the social sciences: How to plan, create, and execute research using experiments.* SAGE.

Condello, G., Capranica, L., Doupona, M., Varga, K., & Burk, V. (2019). Dual-career through the elite university student-athletes' lenses: The international FISU-EAS survey. *PloS One, 14*(10), e0223278. https:// doi.org/10.1371/journal.pone.0223278

Conway, M. (2021). Online extremism and terrorism research ethics: Researcher safety, informed consent, and the need for tailored guidelines. *Terrorism and Political Violence, 33*(2), 367–80. https://doi .org/10.1080/09546553.2021.1880235

Coomber, R. (1997). Using the internet for survey research. *Sociological Research Online, 2*(2), 1–14. http://doi.org/10.5153/sro.73

Cooper, I. D. (2015). Bibliometrics basics. *Journal of the Medical Library Association: JMLA, 103*(4), 217–18. https://doi.org/10.3163/1536 -5050.103.4.013

Cork, A., Everson, R., Levine, M., & Koschate, M. (2020). Using computational techniques to study social influence online. *Group Processes & Intergroup Relations, 23*(6), 808–26. https://doi.org/10 .1177/1368430220937354

Cornesse, C., & Bosnjak, M. (2018). Is there an association between survey characteristics and representativeness? A meta-analysis. *Survey Research Methods, 12*(1), 1–13. https://doi.org/10.18148/srm/2018.v12i1.7205

Corple, D. J., & Linabary, J. R. (2020). From data points to people: Feminist situated ethics in online big data research. *International Journal of Social Research Methodology, 23*(2), 155–68. https://doi.org /10.1080/13645579.2019.1649832

Costello, L., McDermott, M.-L., & Wallace, R. (2017). Netnography: Range of practices, misperceptions, and missed opportunities. *International Journal of Qualitative Methods, 16*(1), 160940691770064. https://doi.org/10.1177/1609406917700647

Crawford, S., Hokke, S., Nicholson, J. M., Zion, L., Lucke, J., Keyzer, P., & Hackworth, N. (2019). 'It's not black and white': Public health researchers' and ethics committees. Perceptions of engaging research participants online. *Internet Research, 29*(1), 123–43. https://doi.org /10.1108/IntR-07-2017-0278

Crump, M. J., McDonnell, J. V., & Gureckis, T. M. (2013). Evaluating Amazon's Mechanical Turk as a tool for experimental behavioral

research. *PloS One*, 8(3), e57410. https://doi.org/10.1371/journal.pone
.0057410

Daikeler, J., Bošnjak, M., & Lozar Manfreda, K. (2020). Web versus other
survey modes: An updated and extended meta-analysis comparing
response rates. *Journal of Survey Statistics and Methodology*, 8(3),
513–39. https://doi.org/10.1093/jssam/smz008

Deacon, D., Pickering, M., Golding, P., & Murdock, G. (2021).
*Researching communications: A practical guide to methods in media
and cultural analysis*. Bloomsbury Publishing USA.

De Bruijne, M., & Wijnant, A. (2013). Comparing survey results obtained
via mobile devices and computers: An experiment with a mobile web
survey on a heterogeneous group of mobile devices versus a computer-
assisted web survey. *Social Science Computer Review*, 31(4), 482–504.
https://doi.org/10.1177/0894439313483976

De Leeuw, J. R., & Motz, B. A. (2016). Psychophysics in a Web browser?
Comparing response times collected with JavaScript and Psychophysics
Toolbox in a visual search task. *Behavior Research Methods*, 48(1),
1–12. https://doi.org/10.3758/s13428-015-0567-2

De Leyn, T., De Wolf, R., Vanden Abeele, M., & De Marez, L. (2022).
In-between child's play and teenage pop culture: Tweens, TikTok &
privacy. *Journal of Youth Studies*, 25(8), 1108–25. https://doi.org/10
.1080/13676261.2021.1939286

Demant, J., Bakken, S. A., Oksanen, A., & Gunnlaugsson, H. (2019).
Drug dealing on Facebook, Snapchat and Instagram: A qualitative
analysis of novel drug markets in the Nordic countries. *Drug and
Alcohol Review*, 38(4), 377–85. https://doi.org/10.1111/dar.12932

Deng, S., Tong, J., Lin, Y., Li, H., & Liu, Y. (2019). Motivating scholars'
responses in academic social networking sites: An empirical study on
ResearchGate Q&A behavior. *Information Processing & Management*,
56(6), 102082. https://doi.org/10.1016/j.ipm.2019.102082

de Villiers, C., Farooq, M. B., & Molinari, M. (2021). Qualitative
research interviews using online video technology – challenges and
opportunities. *Meditari Accountancy Research*, 30(6), 1764–82.
https://doi.org/10.1108/MEDAR-03-2021-1252

Dezuanni, M., Reddan, B., Rutherford, L., & Schoonens, A. (2022).
Selfies and shelfies on #bookstagram and #booktok – social media
and the mediation of Australian teen reading. *Learning, Media and
Technology*, 47(3), 355–72. https://doi.org/10.1080/17439884.2022
.2068575

Di Franco, G., & Santurro, M. (2021). Machine learning, artificial neural
networks and social research. *Quality & Quantity*, 55(3), 1007–25.
https://doi.org/10.1007/s11135-020-01037-y

Dillman, D. A., Smyth, J. A., & Christian, L. A. (2014). *Internet, phone,
mail, and mixed–mode surveys: The tailored design method*. Wiley.

Duffy, B. E., & Pooley, J. D. (2017). 'Facebook for academics': The convergence of self-branding and social media logic on Academia.edu . *Social Media+ Society, 3*(1), 2056305117696523. https://doi.org/10 .1177/2056305117696523

Duflo, E., & Banerjee, A. (2017). *Handbook of field experiments*. North Holland.

Duggan, M. (2017). Questioning 'digital ethnography' in an era of ubiquitous computing. *Geography Compass, 11*(5), e12313. https://doi .org/10.1111/gec3.12313

Edney, S. M., Park, S. H., Tan, L., Chua, X. H., Dickens, B. S. L., Rebello, S. A., . . . van Dam, R. M. (2022). Advancing understanding of dietary and movement behaviours in an Asian population through real-time monitoring: Protocol of the Continuous Observations of Behavioural Risk Factors in Asia study (COBRA). *Digital Health, 8,* 20552076221110534. https://doi.org/10.1177/20552076221110534

Edwards, A., Fitzgerald, R., Beneito-Montagut, R., & Housley, W. (Eds.). (2022). *The SAGE Handbook of Digital Society*. SAGE.

Eichhorn, J. (2022). *Survey research and sampling*. SAGE.

Elgesem, D., Enjolras, B., Ess, C. M., Larson, A. O., Luders, M., Prabhu, R., Segadal, K., Staksrud, E., & Steen-Johnsen, K. (2015). *Internet research ethics*. Cappelen Damm Akademisk.

Ellis, D., Foster, A., & Shehata, A. M. K. (2017). Changing styles of informal academic communication in the age of the Web: Orthodox, moderate and heterodox responses. *Journal of Documentation, 73*(5), 825–42. https://doi.org/10.1108/JD-06-2016-0083

Ess, C. M. (2002). Ethical decision-making and internet research: Recommendations from the AoIR ethics working committee. *Association of Internet Researchers Ethics Working Committee.* http:// www.aoir.org/reports/ethics.pdf

Ess, C. M. (2020). Internet research ethics and social media. In R. Iphofen (Ed.), *Handbook of research ethics and scientific integrity* (pp. 283–303). Springer International Publishing.

Ess, C. M., & Association of Internet Researchers Working Committee (2002). *Ethical decision-making and internet research: Recommendations from the AOIR Ethics Working Committee.* AOIR.

Evans, J. R., & Mathur, A. (2018). The value of online surveys: A look back and a look ahead. *Internet Research, 28*(4), 854–87. https://doi .org/10.1108/IntR-03-2018-0089

Fielding, N. G., Lee, R. M., & Blank, G. (Eds.). (2016). *The SAGE Handbook of online research methods* (2nd ed.). SAGE Publications Ltd.

Fileborn, B. (2016). Participant recruitment in an online era: A reflection on ethics and identity. *Research Ethics, 12*(2), 97–115. https://doi.org /10.1177/1747016115604150 franzke, a. s., Bechmann, A., Zimmer, M., Ess, C. M., & Association of Internet Researchers. (2020). *Internet research: Ethical Guidelines 3.0.* Association of Internet Researchers. https://aoir.org/reports/ethics3.pdf

Fricker, R. D. (2016). Sampling methods for online surveys. In N. G. Fielding, R. M. Lee, & G. Blank (Eds.), *The SAGE handbook of online research methods* (pp. 184–202). SAGE.

Fritz, R. L., & Vandermause, R. (2018). Data collection via in-depth email interviewing: Lessons from the field. *Qualitative Health Research, 28*(10), 1640–9. https://doi.org/10.1177/1049732316689067

Fuchs, C. (2016). Red scare 2.0. *Journal of Language & Politics, 15*(4), 369–98. https://doi.org/10.1075/jlp.15.4.01fuc

Fuchs, C. (2018). 'Dear Mr. Neo-Nazi, can you please give me your informed consent so that I can quote your fascist tweet?': Questions of social media research ethics in online ideology critique. In G. Meikle (Ed.), *The Routledge companion to media and activism* (pp. 385–94). Routledge.

Fuchs, C. (2021). *Social media: A critical introduction* (3rd ed.). SAGE.

Fuchs, C. (2022). *Digital ethics: Media, communication and society. Volume five.* Routledge.

Fujii, L. A. (2018). *Interviewing in Social Science Research: A Relational Approach.* Routledge. https://doi-org.10.4324/9780203756065

Funke, F. (2016). A web experiment showing negative effects of slider scales compared to visual analogue scales and radio button scales. *Social Science Computer Review, 34*(2), 244–254. https://doi.org/10.1177/0894439315575477

G, N. (2023). How many IoT devices are there in 2023? *TechJury.* https://techjury.net/blog/how-many-iot-devices-are-there/

Gelman, M., Kariv, S., Shapiro, M. D., Silverman, D., & Tadelis, S. (2014). Harnessing naturally occurring data to measure the response of spending to income. *Science, 345*(6193), 212–15. https://doi.org/10.1126/science.1247727

Ghani, N. A., Hamid, S., Targio Hashem, I. A., & Ahmed, E. (2019). Social media big data analytics: A survey. *Computers in Human Behavior, 101,* 417–28. https://doi.org/10.1016/j.chb.2018.08.039

Giaxoglou, K. (2017). Reflections on internet research ethics from language-focused research on web-based mourning: Revisiting the private/public distinction as a language ideology of differentiation. *Applied Linguistics Review, 8*(2–3), 229–50. https://doi.org/10.1515/applirev-2016-1037

Gibson, K. (2022). Bridging the digital divide: Reflections on using WhatsApp instant messenger interviews in youth research. *Qualitative Research in Psychology, 19*(3), 611–31. https://doi.org/10.1080/14780887.2020.1751902

Gobo, G., & Molle, A. (2016). *Doing ethnography* (2nd ed.). SAGE.

Golato, A. (2017). Naturally occurring data. In A. Barron, Y. Gu, & G. Steen (Eds.), *The Routledge Handbook of Pragmatics* (1st ed., pp. 21–6). Routledge. https://doi.org/10.4324/9781315668925-3

Goldstone, R. L., & Lupyan, G. (2016). Discovering psychological principles by mining naturally occurring data sets. *Topics in Cognitive Science*, 8(3), 548–68. https://doi.org/10.1111/tops.12212

Gosling, S. D., & Johnson, J. A. (2010). *Advanced methods for conducting behavioural research online.* American Psychological Association.

Gould, S. J., Cox, A. L., Brumby, D. P., & Wiseman, S. (2015). Home is where the lab is: A comparison of online and lab data from a time-sensitive study of interruption. *Human Computation*, 2(1). https://doi.org/10.15346/hc.v2i1.4

Grabher, G. (2020). Enclosure 4.0: Seizing data, selling predictions, scaling platforms. *Sociologica*, 14(3), 241–65. http://orcid.org/0000-0002-2911-9254

Graham, A., Powell, M. A., Taylor, N., Anderson, D., Fitzgerald, R., United Nations Children's Fund (UNICEF), Southern Cross University. Centre for Children and Young People, University of Otago, & Childwatch International Research Network. (2013). *Ethical research involving children.* UNICEF Office of Research - Innocenti.

Gray, L. M., Wong-Wylie, G., Rempel, G. R., & Cook, K. (2020). Expanding qualitative research interviewing strategies: Zoom video communications. *The Qualitative Report*, 25(5), 1292–301. https://nsuworks.nova.edu/tqr/vol25/iss5/9/

Green, D. P. (2022). *Social science experiments: A hands on introduction.* Cambridge University Press.

Grimmer, J., Roberts, M. E., & Stewart, B. M. (2021). Machine learning for social science: An agnostic approach. *Annual Review of Political Science*, 24, 395–419. https://doi.org/10.1146/annurev-polisci-053119-015921

Gubrium, J. F., Holstein, J. A., Marvasti, A. B., & McKinney, K. D. (Eds.). (2021). *The SAGE handbook of interview research: The complexity of the craft* (2nd ed.). SAGE. https://dx.doi.org/10.4135/9781452218403

Hair, N., Akdevelioglu, D., & Clark, M. (2023). The philosophical and methodological guidelines for ethical online ethnography. *International Journal of Market Research*, 65(1), 12–28. https://doi.org/10.1177/14707853221137459

Hall, O., & Wahab, I. (2021). The use of drones in the spatial social sciences. *Drones*, 5(4), 112. https://doi.org/10.3390/drones5040112

Harris, P., Easterbrook, M., & Horst, J. S. (2021). *Designing and reporting experiments in psychology.* Open University Press.

Hart, T. (2017). Online ethnography. In *The international encyclopedia of communication research methods* (pp. 1–8). John Wiley & Sons, Ltd. https://doi.org/10.1002/9781118901731.iecrm0172

Harvey, O., van Teijlingen, E., & Parrish, M. (2023). Using a range of communication tools to interview a hard-to-reach population. *Sociological Research Online*, 13607804221142212. https://doi.org/10.1177/13607804221142212

Hauser, D. J., & Schwarz, N. (2016). Attentive Turkers: MTurk participants perform better on online attention checks than do subject pool participants. *Behavior Research Methods*, 48(1), 400–7. https://doi.org/10.3758/s13428-015-0578-z

Hawkins, J. (2018). The practical utility and suitability of email interviews in qualitative research. *The Qualitative Report*, 23(2). https://digitalcommons.odu.edu/nursing_fac_pubs/24

Hawkins, R. X. (2015). Conducting real-time multiplayer experiments on the web. *Behavior Research Methods*, 47(4), 966–76. https://doi.org/10.3758/s13428-014-0515-6

Heath, J., Williamson, H., Williams, L., & Harcourt, D. (2018). 'It's just more personal': Using multiple methods of qualitative data collection to facilitate participation in research focusing on sensitive subjects. *Applied Nursing Research*, 43, 30–5. https://doi.org/10.1016/j.apnr.2018.06.015

Heen, M., Lieberman, J. D., & Meithe, T. D. (2014). *A comparison of different online sampling approaches for generating national samples*. University of Nevada. http://hdl.handle.net/20.500.11990/3446

Hennink, M., Hutter, I., & Bailey, A. (2020). *Qualitative Research Methods* (2nd ed.). SAGE.

Hergueux, J., & Jacquemet, N. (2015). Social preferences in the online laboratory: A randomized experiment. *Experimental Economics*, 18(2), 251–83. https://doi.org/10.1007/s10683-014-9400-5

Herman, E., & Nicholas, D. (2019). Scholarly reputation building in the digital age: An activity-specific approach. *El Profesional de la Información*, 28(1), e280102. https://doi.org/10.3145/epi.2019.ene.0

Hewson, C., Vogel, C., & Laurent, D. (2015). *Internet research methods* (2nd ed.). SAGE.

Hillygus, S., Jackson, N., & Young, M. (2014). Professional respondents in non-probability online panels. In M. Callegaro, R. Baker, J. Bethlehem, A. S. Göritz, J. A. Krosnick, & P. J. Lavrakas (Eds.), *Online panel research: A data quality perspective* (pp. 219–37). John Wiley & Sons.

Hine, C. (2015). *Ethnography for the internet*. Bloomsbury.

Hine, C. M. (2000). *Virtual ethnography*. SAGE.

Hine, C. M. (2017). Ethnographies of online communities and social media: Modes, varieties, affordances. In N. G. Fielding, R. M. Lee, &

G. Blank, *The SAGE Handbook of Online Research Methods* (pp. 401–13). SAGE. https://doi.org/10.4135/9781473957992.n23

Hogan, B. (2022). *From social science to data science: Key data collection and analysis skills in Python*. SAGE.

Hooley, T., Marriott, J., & Wellens, J. (2012). *What is online research? Using the internet for social science research*. Bloomsbury.

Howlett, M. (2022). Looking at the 'field' through a Zoom lens: Methodological reflections on conducting online research during a global pandemic. *Qualitative Research*, 22(3), 387–402. https://doi.org/10.1177/1468794120985691

Hugentobler, L. (2022). The Instagram interview: Talking to people about travel experiences across online and offline spaces. *Media and Communication*, 10(3), 247–60. https://doi.org/10.17645/mac.v10i3.5340

Hunsinger, J., Allen, M., & Klastrup, L. (Eds.). (2020). *Second international handbook of internet research*. Springer Dordrecht.

Innocenti, A. (2017). Virtual reality experiments in economics. *Journal of Behavioral and Experimental Economics*, 69, 71–7. https://doi.org/10.1016/j.socec.2017.06.001

Israel, M. (2015). *Research ethics and integrity for social scientists: Beyond regulatory compliance*. London.

James, N., & Busher, H. (2014). Internet interviewing. In J. Gubrium, J. Holstein, A. Marvasti, & K. McKinney, *The SAGE Handbook of Interview Research: The Complexity of the Craft* (pp. 177–92). SAGE. https://doi.org/10.4135/9781452218403.n12

Jandrić, P., Ryberg, T., Knox, J., Lacković, N., Hayes, S., Suoranta, J., Smith, M., Steketee, A., Peters, M., McLaren, P., Ford, D. R., Asher, G., McGregor, C., Stewart, G., Williamson, B., & Gibbons, A. (2019). Postdigital dialogue. *Postdigital Science and Education*, 1(1), 163–89. https://doi.org/10.1007/s42438-018-0011-x

Jennings, R. (2020). This week in TikTok: And the most popular video of the year is. *Vox*. https://www.vox.com/the-goods/2020/12/8/22160034/tiktok-top-100-bella-poarch

Jensen, K. B. (Ed.). (2020). *A handbook of media and communication research: Qualitative and quantitative methodologies*. Routledge.

Johnson, M. R., & Woodcock, J. (2019). The impacts of live streaming and Twitch.tv on the video game industry. *Media, Culture & Society*, 41(5), 670–88. https://doi.org/10.1177/0163443718818363

Jones, K., Perry, M., & Regalado, M. (2023). 'You're on mute': A reflective case study of conducting scenario-based online focus groups on student privacy in higher education. In *SAGE Research Methods: Doing Research Online*. https://doi.org/10.4135/9781529799415

Jordan, K., & Weller, M. (2018). Academics and social networking sites: Benefits, problems and tensions in professional engagement with online networking. *Journal of Interactive Media in Education*, 2018(1). http://dx.doi.org/doi:10.5334/jime.448

Jørgensen, K. M. (2016). The media go-along: Researching mobilities with media at hand. *MedieKultur*, 60, 32–49. https://doi.org/10.7146/mediekultur.v32i60.22429

Jun, E., Hsieh, G., & Reinecke, K. (2017). Types of motivation affect study selection, attention, and dropouts in online experiments. *Proceedings of the ACM on Human-Computer Interaction*, 1(CSCW), 1–15. https://doi.org/10.1145/2766462.2767706

Käihkö, I. (2020). Conflict chatnography: Instant messaging apps, social media and conflict ethnography in Ukraine. *Ethnography*, 21(1), 71–91. https://doi.org/10.1177/1466138118781640

Kang, M., & Chai, K. (2022). Wearable sensing systems for monitoring mental health. *Sensors*, 22(3), 994. https://doi.org/10.3390/s22030994

Kar, A. K., & Dwivedi, Y. K. (2020). Theory building with big data-driven research–Moving away from the 'What' towards the 'Why'. *International Journal of Information Management*, 54, 102205. https://doi.org/10.1016/j.ijinfomgt.2020.102205

Kara, H. (2018). *Research ethics in the real world*. Policy Press.

Karamshuk, D., Shaw, F., Brownlie, J., & Sastry, N. (2017). Bridging big data and qualitative methods in the social sciences: A case study of Twitter responses to high profile deaths by suicide. *Online Social Networks and Media*, 1, 33–43. https://doi.org/10.1016/j.osnem.2017.01.002

Keikhosrokiani, P. (Ed.). (2022). *Handbook of research on consumer behavior change and data analytics in the socio-digital era*. IGI Global.

Keusch, F. (2015). Why do people participate in web surveys? Applying survey participation theory to Internet survey data collection. *Management Review Quarterly*, 65(3), 183–216. https://doi.org/10.1007/s11301-014-0111-y

Keuschnigg, M., Bader, F., & Bracher, J. (2016). Using crowdsourced online experiments to study context-dependency of behavior. *Social Science Research*, 59, 68–82. https://doi.org/10.1016/j.ssresearch.2016.04.014

Khder, M. A. (2021). Web scraping or web crawling: State of art, techniques, approaches and application. *International Journal of Advances in Soft Computing & Its Applications*, 13(3), 144–68. https://doi.org/10.15849/IJASCA.211128.11

Kim, J., Gabriel, U., & Gygax, P. (2019). Testing the effectiveness of the Internet-based instrument PsyToolkit: A comparison between web-based (PsyToolkit) and lab-based (E-Prime 3.0) measurements of response choice and response time in a complex psycholinguistic task.

PloS One, 14(9), e0221802. https://doi.org/10.1371/journal.pone
.0221802

King, N., Horrocks, C., & Brooks, J. (2018). *Interviews in qualitative
research* (2nd ed.). SAGE.

Kirner, K., & Mills, J. (2019a). *Doing ethnographic research*. SAGE.

Kirner, K., & Mills, J. (2019b). *Introduction to ethnographic research*.
SAGE.

Kitchin, R. (2013). Big data and human geography: Opportunities,
challenges and risks. *Dialogues in Human Geography*, 3(3), 262–7.
https://doi.org/10.1177/2043820613513388

Kitchin, R. (2016). Big data—Hype or revolution? In L. Sloan & A.
Quan-Haase (Eds.), *The SAGE Handbook of Social Media Research
Methods* (1st ed., pp. 27–39). SAGE. https://doi.org/10.4135
/9781473983847

Kitchin, R., & Lauriault, T. P. (2015). Small data in the era of big data.
GeoJournal, 80, 463–75.

Kite, J., & Phongsavan, P. (2017). *Insights for conducting real-time
focus groups online using a web conferencing service (6:122)*.
F1000Research. https://doi.org/10.12688/f1000research.10427.2

Kjellberg, S., Haider, J., & Sundin, O. (2016). Researchers' use of social
network sites: A scoping review. *Library & Information Science
Research*, 38(3), 224–34. https://doi.org/10.1016/j.lisr.2016.08.008

Knoke, D., & Yang, S. (2019). *Social network analysis*. SAGE.

Kozinets, R. V. (2010). *Netnography: The marketer's secret weapon. How
social media understanding drives innovation*. NetBase.

Kozinets, R. V. (2019). *Netography: The essential guide to qualitative
social media research* (3rd ed.). SAGE.

Kozinets, R. V. (2022). Immersive netnography: A novel method for
service experience research in virtual reality, augmented reality and
metaverse contexts. *Journal of Service Management*, 34(1), 100–25.
https://doi.org/10.1108/JOSM-12-2021-0481

Kramer, A. D., Guillory, J. E., & Hancock, J. T. (2014). Experimental
evidence of massive-scale emotional contagion through social
networks. *Proceedings of the National Academy of Sciences*, 111(24),
8788–90. https://doi.org/10.1073/pnas.1320040111

Kramer, A. D. I., Guillory, J. E., & Hancock, J. T. (2014). Experimental
evidence of massive-scale emotional contagion through social networks.
Proceedings of the National Academy of Sciences, 111(24), 8788–90.

Kreuter, F., Foster, I., Lane, J., Ghani, R., & Jarmin, R. S. (Eds.). (2020).
*Big data and social science: Data science methods and tools for
research and practice*. CRC Press.

Krouwel, M., Jolly, K., & Greenfield, S. (2019). Comparing Skype (video
calling) and in-person qualitative interview modes in a study of people

with irritable bowel syndrome – an exploratory comparative analysis. *BMC Medical Research Methodology, 19*(1), 219. https://doi.org/10.1186/s12874-019-0867-9

Krueger, R. A., & Casey, M. A. (2015). *Focus groups: A practical guide for applied research* (5th ed.). SAGE.

Krug, S. (2013). *Don't make me think revisited.* New Riders.

Krutka, D. G., & Carpenter, J. P. (2016). Enriching professional learning networks: A framework for identification, reflection, and intention. *TechTrends, 61*(3), 246–52. https://doi.org/10.1007/s11528-016-0141-5

Laaksonen, S.-M., Nelimarkka, M., Tuokko, M., Marttila, M., Kekkonen, A., & Villi, M. (2017). Working the fields of big data: Using big-data-augmented online ethnography to study candidate–candidate interaction at election time. *Journal of Information Technology & Politics, 14*(2), 110–31. https://doi.org/10.1080/19331681.2016.1266981

Laniado, D., Volkovich, Y., Scellato, S., Mascolo, C., & Kaltenbrunner, A. (2018). The impact of geographic distance on online social interactions. *Information Systems Frontiers, 20,* 1203–18. https://doi.org/10.1007/s10796-017-9784-9

LaRose, R., & Tsai, H. Y. S. (2014). Completion rates and non-response error in online surveys: Comparing sweepstakes and pre-paid cash incentives in studies of online behavior. *Computers in Human Behavior, 34,* 110–19. https://doi.org/10.1016/j.chb.2014.01.017

Latzko-Toth, G., Bonneau, C., & Millette, M. (2017). Small data, thick data: Data thickening strategies for social media research. In *The SAGE Handbook of Social Media Research Methods* (pp. 157–72). SAGE. https://doi.org/10.4135/9781529782943

Lavis, A., & Winter, R. (2020). #Online harms or benefits? An ethnographic analysis of the positives and negatives of peer-support around self-harm on social media. *Journal of Child Psychology and Psychiatry, 61*(8), 842–54. https://doi.org/10.1111/jcpp.13245

Lee, J., Oh, S., Dong, H., Wang, F., & Burnett, G. (2019). Motivations for self-archiving on an academic social networking site: A study on ResearchGate. *Journal of the Association for Information Science and Technology, 70*(6), 563–74. https://doi.org/10.1002/asi.24138

Lee, T. B. (2014, June 16). The internet, explained. *Vox.* https://www.vox.com/2014/6/16/18076282/the-internet

Lee, Y. S., Seo, Y. W., & Siemsen, E. (2018). Running behavioral operations experiments using Amazon's Mechanical Turk. *Production and Operations Management, 27*(5), 973–89. https://doi.org/10.1111/poms.12841

Lehdonvirta, V., Oksanen, A., Räsänen, P., & Blank, G. (2021). Social media, web, and panel surveys: Using non-probability samples in social

and policy research. *Policy & Internet, 13*(1), 134–55. https://doi.org
/10.1002/poi3.238

Lewis, S. C., Zamith, R., & Hermida, A. (2013). Content analysis in an
era of big data: A hybrid approach to computational and manual
methods. *Journal of Broadcasting & Electronic Media, 57*(1), 34–52.
https://doi.org/10.1080/08838151.2012.761702

Li, Y., Guan, M., Hammond, P., & Berrey, L. E. (2021). Communicating
COVID-19 information on TikTok: A content analysis of TikTok
videos from official accounts featured in the COVID-19 information
hub. *Health Education Research, 36*(3), 261–71. https://doi.org/10
.1093/her/cyab010

Liao, S. H., Widowati, R., & Lee, C. Y. (2022). Data mining analytics
investigation on TikTok users' behaviors: Social media app
development. *Library Hi Tech.* https://doi.org/10.1108/LHT-08-2022
-0368

Liu, M., & Wronski, L. (2018). Examining completion rates in web
surveys via over 25,000 real-world surveys. *Social Science Computer
Review, 36*(1), 116–24. https://doi.org/10.1177/0894439317695581

LLaudet, E., & Kosuke, I. (2023). *Data analysis for social science.*
Princeton University Press.

Lobe, B., & Morgan, D. L. (2021). Assessing the effectiveness of video-
based interviewing: A systematic comparison of video-conferencing
based dyadic interviews and focus groups. *International Journal of
Social Research Methodology, 24*(3), 301–12. https://doi.org/10.1080
/13645579.2020.1785763

Lobe, B., Morgan, D. L., & Hoffman, K. (2022). A systematic comparison
of in-person and video-based online interviewing. *International
Journal of Qualitative Methods, 21*, 160940692211270. https://doi.org
/10.1177/16094069221127068

Locatelli, E. (2020). Ethics of social media research: State of the debate
and future challenges. In J. Hunsinger, M. M. Allen, & L. Klastrup
(Eds.), *Second international handbook of internet research* (pp.
835–56). Springer Netherlands.

Lucey, B., & Dowling, M. (2023). ChatGPT: Our study shows AI can
produce academic papers good enough for journals – just as some ban
it. *The Conversation.* https://theconversation.com/chatgpt-our-study
-shows-ai-can-produce-academic-papers-good-enough-for-journals-just
-as-some-ban-it-197762

Lugosi, P., & Quinton, S. (2018). More-than-human netnography. *Journal
of Marketing Management, 34*(3–4), 287–313. https://doi.org/10.1080
/0267257X.2018.1431303

Luka, M. E., & Millette, M. (2018). (Re)framing big data: Activating
situated knowledges and a feminist ethics of care in social media

research. *Social Media + Society*, 4(2) 205630511876829. https://doi
.org/10.1177/2056305118768297

Lundström, M., & Lundström, T. P. (2021). Podcast ethnography.
International Journal of Social Research Methodology, 24(3), 289–99.
https://doi.org/10.1080/13645579.2020.1778221

Lupton, D. (2014). 'Feeling better connected': Academics' use of social
media. https://apo.org.au/node/53908

Lupton, D. (2015). *Digital sociology* (1st ed.). Routledge.

Lupton, D. (2016). *Personal data practices in the age of lively data*
(SSRN Scholarly Paper No. 2636709). https://doi.org/10.2139/ssrn
.2636709

Lupton, D., Mewburn, I., & Thomson, P. (2018). *The digital academic.*
Routledge.

Lupton, D., & Williamson, B. (2017). The datafied child: The
dataveillance of children and implications for their rights. *New Media
& Society*, 19(5), 780–94. https://doi.org/10.1177/14614448
16686328

Luzón, M. J., & Pérez-Llantada, C. (2022). *Digital genres in academic
knowledge production and communication: Perspectives and practices.*
Multilingual Matters.

Mackenzie, J. (2017). Identifying informational norms in Mumsnet talk:
A reflexive-linguistic approach to internet research ethics. *Applied
Linguistics Review*, 8(2–3), 293–314. https://doi.org/10.1515/applirev
-2016-1042

Maclin, M. K. (2020). *Experimental design in psychology: A case
approach.* Routledge.

Markham, A., Buchanan, E., & Association of Internet Researchers
Working Committee. (2012). *Ethical decision-making and internet
research: Recommendations from the AOIR Ethics Committee.*

Martins, A. I., Queirós, A., Silva, A. G., & Rocha, N. P. (2015). Usability
evaluation methods: A systematic review. In Saeed, S., Sarwar Bajwa,
I., & Mahmood, Z. (Eds.), *Human factors in software development
and design* (pp. 250–73). IGI Global.

Marwick, A. (2013). Ethnographic and qualitative research on twitter. In
K. Weller, A. Bruns, C. Puschmann, & J. Burgess (Eds.), *Twitter and
society* (pp. 109–22). Peter Lang.

Marzano, M. (2021). Covert research ethics. In R. Iphofen & D.
O'Mathúna (Eds.), *Ethical issues in covert, security and surveillance
research* (pp. 41–53). Emerald Publishing Limited.

Mathysen, D., & Glorieux, I. (2021). Integrating virtual reality in
qualitative research methods: Making a case for the VR-assisted
interview. *Methodological Innovations*, 14(2), 20597991211030776.
https://doi.org/10.1177/20597991211030778

Matthews, K. L., Baird, M., & Duchesne, G. (2018). Using online meeting software to facilitate geographically dispersed focus groups for health workforce research. *Qualitative Health Research*, 28(10), 1621–8. https://doi.org/10.1177/1049732318782167

McFarland, D. A., Lewis, K., & Goldberg, A. (2016). Sociology in the era of big data: The ascent of forensic social science. *The American Sociologist*, 47, 12–35. https://doi.org/10.1007/s12108-015-9291-8

McInroy, L. B. (2016). Pitfalls, potentials, and ethics of online survey research: LGBTQ and other marginalized and hard-to-access youths. *Social Work Research*, 40(2), 83–94. https://doi.org/10.1093/swr/svw005

Meishar-Tal, H., & Pieterse, E. (2017). Why do academics use academic social networking sites? *International Review of Research in Open and Distributed Learning*, 18(1), 1–22. https://doi.org/10.19173/irrodl.v18i1.2643

Menzie, L. (2022). Stacys, Beckys, and Chads: The construction of femininity and hegemonic masculinity within incel rhetoric. *Psychology & Sexuality*, 13(1), 69–85. https://doi.org/10.1080/19419899.2020.1806915

Mewburn, I., & Clews, S. (2023). *Be visible or vanish: Engage, influence, and ensure your research has impact*. Routledge.

Mirea, M., Wang, V., & Jung, J. (2019). The not so dark side of the darknet: A qualitative study. *Security Journal*, 32(2), 102–18. https://doi.org/10.1057/s41284-018-0150-5

Mockler, N. (2020a). Ten years of print media coverage of NAPLAN: A corpus-assisted assessment. *Australian Review of Applied Linguistics*, 43(2), 117–44. https://doi.org/10.1075/aral.19047.moc

Mockler, N. (2020b). Discourses of teacher quality in the Australian print media 2014–2017: A corpus-assisted analysis. *Discourse: Studies in the Cultural Politics of Education*, 41(6), 854–70. https://doi.org/10.1080/01596306.2018.1553849

Møller, K., & Robards, B. (2019). Walking through, going along and scrolling back: Ephemeral mobilities in digital ethnography. *Nordicom Review*, 40(s1), 95–109. https://doi.org/10.2478/nor-2019-0016

Moss, A., & Litman, L. (2018). After the bot scare: Understanding what's been happening with data collection on MTurk and how to stop it. *CloudResearch Blog*. https://www.cloudresearch.com/resources/blog/after-the-bot-scare-understanding-whats-been-happening-with-data-collection-on-mturk-and-how-to-stop-it/

Muise, D., & Pan, J. (2019). Online field experiments. *Asian Journal of Communication*, 29(3), 217–34. https://doi.org/10.1080/01292986.2018.1453850

Müller, J., Fàbregues, S., Guenther, E. A., & Romano, M. J. (2019). Using sensors in organizational research—Clarifying rationales and validation challenges for mixed methods. *Frontiers in Psychology, 10,* 1188. https://doi.org/10.3389/fpsyg.2019.01188

Mullinix, K. J., Leeper, T. J., Druckman, J. N., & Freese, J. (2015). The generalizability of survey experiments. *Journal of Experimental Political Science, 2*(2), 109–38. https://doi.org/10.1017/XPS.2015.19

Muscanell, N., & Utz, S. (2017). Social networking for scientists: An analysis on how and why academics use ResearchGate. *Online Information Review, 41*(5), 744–59. https://doi.org/10.1108/OIR-07-2016-0185

Namey, E., Guest, G., O'Regan, A., Godwin, C. L., Taylor, J., & Martinez, A. (2020). How does mode of qualitative data collection affect data and cost? Findings from a quasi-experimental study. *Field Methods, 32*(1), 58–74. https://doi.org/10.1177/1525822X19886839

Naslund, J. A., Grande, S. W., Aschbrenner, K. A., & Elwyn, G. (2014). Naturally occurring peer support through social media: The experiences of individuals with severe mental illness using YouTube. *PLOS ONE, 9*(10), e110171. https://doi.org/10.1371/journal.pone.0110171

Ng, I. C., & Wakenshaw, S. Y. (2017). The internet-of-things: Review and research directions. *International Journal of Research in Marketing, 34*(1), 3–21. https://doi.org/10.1016/j.ijresmar.2016.11.003

Nicholas, D., Herman, E., Xu, J., Boukacem-Zeghmouri, C., Abdullah, A., Watkinson, A., . . . Rodríguez-Bravo, B. (2018). Early career researchers' quest for reputation in the digital age. *Journal of Scholarly Publishing, 49*(4), 375–96. https://doi.org/10.3138/jsp.49.4.01

Ogunniye, G., & Kokciyan, N. (2023). A survey on understanding and representing privacy requirements in the Internet-of-Things. *Journal of Artificial Intelligence Research, 76,* 163–92. https://doi.org/10.1613/jair.1.14000

Oreg, A., & Babis, D. (2023). Digital ethnography in third sector research. *VOLUNTAS: International Journal of Voluntary and Nonprofit Organizations, 34*(1), 12–19. https://doi.org/10.1007/s11266-021-00397-9

Ortmann, A. (2019). Deception. In A. Schram & A. Ule (Eds.), *Handbook of Research Methods and Applications in Experimental Economics* (pp. 28–38). Edward Elgar.

Ozono, H., & Nakama, D. (2022). Effects of experimental situation on group cooperation and individual performance: Comparing laboratory and online experiments. *PLoS One, 17*(4): e0267251. https://doi.org/10.1371/journal.pone.0267251

Palan, S., & Schitter, C. (2018). Prolific. ac—A subject pool for online experiments. *Journal of Behavioral and Experimental Finance*, *17*, 22–7. https://doi.org/10.1016/j.jbef.2017.12.004

Paolacci, G., & Chandler, J. (2014). Inside the Turk: Understanding mechanical Turk as a participant pool. *Current Directions in Psychological Science*, *23*(3), 184–8. https://doi.org/10.1177/0963721414531598

Paoli, A. D., & D'Auria, V. (2021). Digital ethnography: A systematic literature review. *Italian Sociological Review*, *11*(4S), Article 4S. https://doi.org/10.13136/isr.v11i4S.434

Paoli, A. D., & Masullo, G. (2022). The desexualization of society. A digital ethnography on the asexual community. *Italian Journal of Sociology of Education*, *14*(3), 153–72. https://doi.org/10.14658/PUPJ-IJSE-2022-3-7

Parigi, P., Santana, J. J., & Cook, K. S. (2017). Online field experiments: Studying social interactions in context. *Social Psychology Quarterly*, *80*(1), 1–19. https://doi.org/10.1177/0190272516680842

Pedersen, M. J., & Nielsen, C. V. (2016). Improving survey response rates in online panels: Effects of low-cost incentives and cost-free text appeal interventions. *Social Science Computer Review*, *34*(2), 229–43. https://doi.org/10.1177/0894439314563916

Peer, E., Brandimarte, L., Samat, S., & Acquisti, A. (2017). Beyond the Turk: Alternative platforms for crowdsourcing behavioral research. *Journal of Experimental Social Psychology*, *70*, 153–63. https://doi.org/10.1016/j.jesp.2017.01.006

Penner, A. M., & Dodge, K. A. (2019). Using administrative data for social science and policy. *RSF: The Russell Sage Foundation Journal of the Social Sciences*, *5*(2), 1–18. https://doi.org/10.7758/RSF.2019.5.2.01

Perry, S. M. (2018). *Maximising social science research through publicly accessible data sets*. IGI Global.

Petrovčič, A., Petrič, G., & Manfreda, K. L. (2016). The effect of email invitation elements on response rate in a web survey within an online community. *Computers in Human Behavior*, *56*, 320–9. https://doi.org/10.1016/j.chb.2015.11.025

Pickard, M. D., & Roster, C. A. (2020). Using computer automated systems to conduct personal interviews: Does the mere presence of a human face *inhibit disclosure? Computers in Human Behavior*, *105*, 106197. https://doi.org/10.1016/j.chb.2019.106197

Pihlaja, S. (2017). More than fifty shades of grey: Copyright on social network sites. *Applied Linguistics Review*, *8*(2–3), 213–28. https://doi.org/10.1515/applirev-2016-1036

Pink, S., Horst, H., Postill, J., Hjorth, L., Lewis, T., & Tacchi, J. (2016). *Digital ethnography: Principles and practice.* SAGE.

Pitcan, M., Marwick, A. E., & boyd, D. (2018). Performing a vanilla self: Respectability politics, social class, and the digital world. *Journal of Computer-Mediated Communication, 23*(3), 163–79. https://doi.org/10.1093/jcmc/zmy008

Piwowar, H., Priem, J., Larivière, V., Alperin, J. P., Matthias, L., Norlander, B., . . . Haustein, S. (2018). The state of OA: A large-scale analysis of the prevalence and impact of open access articles. *PeerJ, 6,* e4375. https://peerj.com/articles/4375/

Platt, J. (2014). The history of the interview. In J. Gubrium, J. Holstein, A. Marvasti, & K. McKinney, *The SAGE Handbook of interview research: The complexity of the craft* (pp. 9–26). SAGE. https://doi.org/10.4135/9781452218403.n2

Poarch, B. (2020). *M to the B - Millie B.* https://www.tiktok.com/@bellapoarch/video/6862153058223197445?embed_source=121331973%2C71011723%2C120811592%2C120810756%3Bnull%3Bembed_blank&refer=embed&referer_url=www.vox.com%2Fthe-goods%2F2020%2F12%2F8%2F22160034%2Ftiktok-top-100-bella-poarch&referer_video_id=6862153058223197445

Pooley, J. (2022). Surveillance publishing. *The Journal of Electronic Publishing, 25*(1). https://doi.org/10.3998/jep.1874

Popping, R. (2017). Online tools for content analysis. In N. G. Fielding, R. M. Lee, & G. Blank (Eds.). *The SAGE handbook of online research methods* (pp. 329–43). SAGE.

Pronk, T., Wiers, R. W., Molenkamp, B., & Murre, J. (2020). Mental chronometry in the pocket? Timing accuracy of web applications on touchscreen and keyboard devices. *Behavior Research Methods, 52*(3), 1371–82. https://doi.org/10.3758/s13428-019-01321-2

Przybylski, L. (2020). *Hybrid ethnography: Online, offline and in between.* SAGE.

Puschmann, C. (2019). An end to the wild west of social media research: A response to Axel Bruns. *Information, Communication & Society, 22*(11), 1582–9, https://doi.org/10.1080/1369118X.2019.1646300

Quan-Haase, A., & Sloan, L. (Eds.). (2022). *The SAGE handbook of social media research methods.* SAGE.

Radford, M. L., Kitzie, V., Mikitish, S., Floegel, D., Radford, G. P., & Connaway, L. S. (2020). 'People are reading your work', scholarly identity and social networking sites. *Journal of Documentation, 76*(6), 1233–60. https://doi.org/10.1108/JD-04-2019-0074

Ravert, R. D., Gomez-Scott, J., & Donnellan, M. B. (2015). Equivalency of paper versus tablet computer survey data. *Educational Researcher, 44*(5), 308–10. https://doi.org/10.3102/0013189X15592845

Reips, U.-D. (2007). The methodology of internet-based experiments. In A. Joinson, K. McKenna, T. Postmes, & U.-D. Reips (Eds.), *The Oxford Handbook of Internet Psychology* (pp. 373–90). Oxford University Press.

Reips, U.-D. (2022). *Web-based research in psychology*. Hogrefe Publishing.

Revilla, M., Toninelli, D., Ochoa, C., & Loewe, G. (2015). Do online access panels need to adapt surveys for mobile devices? *Internet Research, 26*(5), 1209–27. https://doi.org/10.1108/IntR-02-2015-0032

Reynolds, N., & Quinton, S. (2018). *Understanding research in the digital age*. SAGE.

Robards, B., & Lincoln, S. (2019). Social media scroll back method. In *Sage Research Methods*. SAGE. https://doi.org/10.4135/9781526421036851495

Roberts, J. K., Pavlakis, A. E., & Richards, M. P. (2021). It's more complicated than it seems: Virtual qualitative research in the COVID-19 era. *International Journal of Qualitative Methods, 20* 160940692110029. https://doi.org/10.1177/16094069211002959

Robinson, J., Rosenzweig, C., Moss, A. J., & Litman, L. (2019). Tapped out or barely tapped? Recommendations for how to harness the vast and largely unused potential of the Mechanical Turk participant pool. *PloS One, 14*(12), e0226394. https://doi.org/10.1371/journal.pone.0226394

Rogers, R. (2019). *Doing digital methods*. SAGE.

Roulston, K. (2012). The pedagogy of interviewing. In J. Gubrium, J. Holstein, A. Marvasti, & K. McKinney, *The SAGE Handbook of Interview Research: The Complexity of the Craft* (pp. 61–74). SAGE. https://doi.org/10.4135/9781452218403.n5

Rule, E., Wagner, W. E., & Gillespie, B. J. (2016). *The practice of survey research*. SAGE.

Russell, B., & Purcell, J. (2009). *Online research essentials: Designing and implementing research studies*. Wiley.

Saarijärvi, M., & Bratt, E.-L. (2021). When face-to-face interviews are not possible: Tips and tricks for video, telephone, online chat, and email interviews in qualitative research. *European Journal of Cardiovascular Nursing, 20*, 392–6. https://doi.org/10.1093/eurjcn/zvab038

Saleh, A., & Bista, K. (2017). Examining factors impacting online survey response rates in educational research: Perceptions of graduate students. *Journal of Multi-Disciplinary Evaluation, 13*(29), 63–74. https://journals.sfu.ca/jmde/index.php/jmde_1/article/view/487

Salganik, M. J. (2019). *Bit by bit: Social research in the digital age*. Princeton University Press.

Salmons, J. (2015). Designing and conducting research with online interviews. In J. Salmons (Ed.), *Cases in Online Interview Research* (pp. 1–30). SAGE Publications, Inc. https://doi.org/10.4135/9781506335155.n1

Sarwar, A., Imran, M. K., Akhtar, N., & Fatima, T. (2022). Does social media usage boost career prospects of women: An exploratory study in the academia. *Kybernetes*. https://doi.org/10.1108/K-04-2021-0294

Sauter, M., Draschkow, D., & Mack, W. (2020). Building, hosting and recruiting: A brief introduction to running behavioral experiments online. *Brain Sciences*, *10*(4), 251. https://doi.org/10.3390/brainsci10040251

Saxena, S., Lange, E., & Fink, L. (2022). Towards efficient calibration for webcam eye-tracking in online experiments. *2022 Symposium on Eye Tracking Research and Applications*, *27*, 1–7. https://doi.org/10.1145/3517031.3529645

Schäfer, M. T., & van Ess, K. (Eds.). (2017). *The datafied society. Studying culture through data*. Amsterdam University Press.

Schuldt, B. A., & Totten, J. W. (1994). Electronic mail vs. mail survey response rates. *Marketing Research*, *6*(1), 36–9.

Schulz, P., Kreft, A. K., Touquet, H., & Martin, S. (2022). Self-care for gender-based violence researchers – beyond bubble baths and chocolate pralines. *Qualitative Research*, *23*(5), 1461–1480. https://doi.org/10.1177/14687941221087868

Seligmann, L. J., & Estes, B. P. (2020). Innovations in ethnographic methods. *American Behavioral Scientist*, *64*(2), 176–97. https://doi.org/10.1177/0002764219859640

Selwyn, N. (2018). *What is digital sociology?* John Wiley & Sons.

Shannon, B. (2022). Networked publics and online sex(uality) education. In B. Shannon (Ed.), *Sex(uality) education for trans and gender diverse youth in Australia* (pp. 155–78). Springer International Publishing. https://doi.org/10.1007/978-3-030-92446-1_9

Sharp, M., & Shannon, B. (2020). Becoming non-binary: An exploration of gender work in Tumblr. In D. N. Farris, D. R. Compton, & A. P. Herrera (Eds.), *Gender, sexuality and race in the digital age* (pp. 137–50). Springer International Publishing. https://doi.org/10.1007/978-3-030-29855-5_8

Shelton, S., & Jones, A. (2022). Advantages of and considerations for conducting online focus groups. In *SAGE Research Methods: Doing Research Online*. SAGE. https://doi.org/10.4135/9781529601824

Silver, D. (2000). Looking backwards, looking forwards: Cyberculture studies 1990–2000. In D. Gauntlett (Ed.), *Web studies. Rewiring media studies for the digital age* (pp. 19–30). Arnold.

Simcox, T., & Fiez, J. A. (2014). Collecting response times using amazon mechanical Turk and adobe flash. *Behavior Research Methods*, 46(1), 95–111. https://doi.org/10.3758/s13428-013-0345-y

Similarweb. (2023). *Top websites ranking.* https://www.similarweb.com/top-websites/

Singh, L. (2020). A systematic review of higher education academics' use of microblogging for professional development: Case of Twitter. *Open Education Studies*, 2(1), 66–81. https://doi.org/10.1515/edu-2020-0102

Sipes, J. B. A., Roberts, L. D., & Mullan, B. (2022). Voice-only Skype for use in researching sensitive topics: A research note. *Qualitative Research in Psychology*, 19(1), 204–20. https://doi.org/10.1080/14780887.2019.1577518

Smith, D. R., & Watson, R. (2016). Career development tips for today's nursing academic: Bibliometrics, altmetrics and social media. *Journal of Advanced Nursing*, 72(11), 2654–61. https://doi.org/10.1111/jan.13067

Srnicek, N. (2016). *Platform capitalism.* Wiley.

Stapleton, C. (2013). The Smart(phone) way to collect survey data. *Survey Practice*, 6(2), 1–8. https://doi.org/10.29115/SP-2013-0011

Stedman, R. C., Connelly, N. A., Heberlein, T. A., Decker, D. J., & Allred, S. B. (2019). The end of the (research) world as we know it? Understanding and coping with declining response rates to mail surveys. *Society & Natural Resources*, 32(10), 1139–54. https://doi.org/10.1080/08941920.2019.1587127

Stewart, D. W., & Shamdasani, P. (2017). Online focus groups. *Journal of Advertising*, 46(1), 48–60. https://doi.org/10.1080/00913367.2016.1252288

Stieglitz, S., Mirbabaie, M., Ross, B., & Neuberger, C. (2018). Social media analytics – challenges in topic discovery, data collection, and data preparation. *International Journal of Information Management*, 39, 156–68. https://doi.org/10.1016/j.ijinfomgt.2017.12.002

Struminskaya, B., Lugtig, P., Keusch, F., & Höhne, J. K. (2020). Augmenting surveys with data from sensors and apps: Opportunities and challenges. *Social Science Computer Review*, 0894439320979951. https://doi.org/10.1177/0894439320979951

Struminskaya, B., Weyandt, K., & Bosnjak, M. (2015). The effects of questionnaire completion using mobile devices on data quality. Evidence from a probability-based general population panel. *Methods, Data, Analyses*, 9(2), 261–92. https://doi.org/10.12758/mda.2015.014

Sugimoto, C. R., Work, S., Larivière, V., & Haustein, S. (2017). Scholarly use of social media and altmetrics: A review of the literature. *Journal of the Association for Information Science and Technology*, 68(9), 2037–62. https://doi.org/10.1002/asi.23833

Sugiura, L., Wiles, R., & Pope, C. (2017). Ethical challenges in online research: Public/private perceptions. *Research Ethics*, *13*(3–4), 184–99. https://doi.org/10.1177/1747016116650720

Sun, M., & Jiang, L. C. (2022). Linking social features of fitness apps with physical activity among Chinese users: Evidence from self-reported and self-tracked behavioral data. *Information Processing & Management*, *59*(6), 103096. https://doi.org/10.1016/j.ipm.2022.103096

Suomela, T., Chee, F., Berendt, B., & Rockwell, G. (2019). Applying an ethics of care to internet research: Gamergate and digital humanities. *Digital Studies/Le champ numérique*, *9*(1), 4. http://doi.org/10.16995/dscn.302

Tarnoff, B. (2022). *Internet for the people*. Verso.

Thatcher, J. (2014). Big data, big questions| living on fumes: Digital footprints, data fumes, and the limitations of spatial big data. *International Journal of Communication*, *8*, 1765–83. https://ijoc.org/index.php/ijoc/article/view/2174/1158

Thelwall, M., & Nevill, T. (2021). Is research with qualitative data more prevalent and impactful now? Interviews, case studies, focus groups and ethnographies. *Library & Information Science Research*, *43*(2), 101094. https://doi.org/10.1016/j.lisr.2021.101094

Third, A., Bellerose, D., Dawkins, U., Keltie, E., & Pihl, K. (2015). Children's rights in the digital age. *Young and Well Cooperative Research Centre*, *16*. http://www.uws.edu.au/__data/assets/pdf_file/0003/753447/Childrens-rights-in-the-digital-age.pdf

Thompson, A., Stringfellow, L., Maclean, M., & Nazzal, A. (2021). Ethical considerations and challenges for using digital ethnography to research vulnerable populations. *Journal of Business Research*, *124*, 676–83. https://doi.org/10.1016/j.jbusres.2020.02.025

Thunberg, S., & Arnell, L. (2022). Pioneering the use of technologies in qualitative research – A research review of the use of digital interviews. *International Journal of Social Research Methodology*, *25*(6), 757–68. https://doi.org/10.1080/13645579.2021.1935565

Toepoel, V. (2016). *Doing surveys online*. SAGE.

Toepoel, V., & Lugtig, P. (2015). Online surveys are mixed-device surveys. Issues associated with the use of different (mobile) devices in web surveys. *Methods, Data, Analyses*, *9*(2), 155–62. https://doi.org/10.12758/mda.2015.009

Toninelli, D., & Revilla, M. (2016). Smartphones vs PCs: Does the device affect the web survey experience and the measurement error for sensitive topics? A replication of the Mavletova & Couper's 2013 experiment. *Survey Research Methods*, *10*(2), 153–69. https://doi.org/10.18148/srm/2016.v10i2.6274

Town, P., & Thabtah, F. (2019). Data analytics tools: A user perspective. *Journal of Information & Knowledge Management*, *18*(1), 1950002. https://doi.org/10.1142/S0219649219500023

Tremblay, L., Dean, S., & Martineau, P. (2022). Conducting online focus groups: Challenges and opportunities. In *SAGE Research Methods: Doing Research Online*. SAGE. https://doi.org/10.4135/9781529602951

Tunçalp, D., & Lê, P. L. (2014). (Re)Locating boundaries: A systematic review of online ethnography. *Journal of Organizational Ethnography*, 3, 59–79. https://doi.org/10.1108/JOE-11-2012-0048

Turrell, A., Speigner, B. J., Djumalieva, J., Copple, D., & Thurgood, J. (2019). *Transforming Naturally Occurring Text Data into Economic Statistics: The Case of Online Job Vacancy Postings (No. w25837)*. National Bureau of Economic Research. https://doi.org/10.3386/w25837

Tuttas, C. A. (2015). Lessons learned using web conference technology for online focus group interviews. *Qualitative Health Research*, 25(1), 122–33. https://doi.org/10.1177/1049732314549602

Tyagi, A. K., & Shamila, M. (2019, February 26–28). Spy in the crowd: How user's privacy is getting affected with the integration of Internet of thing's devices. In *Proceedings of International Conference on Sustainable Computing in Science, Technology and Management (SUSCOM)*. Amity University Rajasthan, Jaipur, India. http://dx.doi.org/10.2139/ssrn.3356268

Udupa, S. (2019). Nationalism in the digital age: Fun as a metapractice of extreme speech. *International Journal of Communication*, 3143–63. https://doi.org/10.5282/ubm/epub.69633

Underwood, M. (2017). Exploring the social lives of image and performance enhancing drugs: An online ethnography of the Zyzz fandom of recreational bodybuilders. *International Journal of Drug Policy*, 39, 78–85. https://doi.org/10.1016/j.drugpo.2016.08.012

UNESCO. (2020). Open access to facilitate research and information on COVID-19. https://en.unesco.org/covid19/communicationinformationresponse/opensolutions

Van Mol, C. (2017). Improving web survey efficiency: The impact of an extra reminder and reminder content on web survey response. *International Journal of Social Research Methodology*, 20(4), 317–27. https://doi.org/10.1080/13645579.2016.1185255

Veltri, G. A. (2019). *Digital social research*. Polity Press.

Vieira, L. N., O'Hagan, M., & O'Sullivan, C. (2021). Understanding the societal impacts of machine translation: A critical review of the literature on medical and legal use cases. *Information, Communication & Society*, 24(11), 1515–32. https://doi.org/10.1080/1369118X.2020.1776370

W3C. (2022). *WCAG 2 overview*. https://www.w3.org/WAI/standards-guidelines/wcag/

Wang, D., & Liu, S. (2021). Doing ethnography on social media: A methodological reflection on the study of online groups in China.

Qualitative Inquiry, 27(8–9), 977–87. https://doi.org/10.1177
/10778004211014610

Wang, J. Y., & Kitsis, E. A. (2013). Tangling the web: Deception in online
research. *American Journal of Bioethics*, *13*(11), 59–61. https://doi.org
/10.1080/15265161.2013.840868

Webb, L. (2017). Online research methods, qualitative. In *The
International Encyclopedia of Communication Research Methods*
(pp. 1339–46). John Wiley & Sons. https://doi.org/10.1002
/9781118901731.iecrm0173

Ward, M. K., & Meade, A. W. (2018). Applying social psychology to
prevent careless responding during online surveys. *Applied Psychology*,
67(2), 231–263. https://doi.org/10.1111/apps.12118

Weller, M. (2011). *The Digital Scholar: How technology is
transforming scholarly practice*. Bloomsbury. https://doi.org/10.5040
/9781849666275

Wells, T. (2015). What market researchers should know about mobile
surveys. *International Journal of Market Research*, *57*(4), 521–32.
https://doi.org/10.2501/IJMR-2015-045

Wells, T., Bailey, J. T., & Link, M. W. (2014). Comparison of smartphone
and online computer survey administration. *Social Science Computer
Review*, *32*(2), 238–55. https://doi.org/10.1177/0894439313505829

Werner, A. (2020). Organizing music, organizing gender: Algorithmic
culture and spotify recommendations. *Popular Communication*, *18*(1),
78–90. https://doi.org/10.1080/15405702.2020.1715980

Whitaker, E. M., & Atkinson, P. (2023). *Ethnography explorations:
Surrender and Resistence*. Routledge.

Wiersma, W. (2012). *From web–forms to virtual worlds: Opportunities
and challenges posed by four types of online experiment*. Oxford
Internet Institute.

Wilke, C. O. (2019). *Fundamentals of data visualization: A primer on
making informative and compelling figures*. O'Reilly Media.

Wilkerson, J. M., Iantaffi, A., Grey, J. A., Bockting, W. O., & Rosser, B.
R. S. (2014). Recommendations for internet-based qualitative health
research with hard-to-reach populations. *Qualitative Health Research*,
24(4), 561–74. https://doi.org/10.1177/1049732314524635

Willemsen, R. F., Aardoom, J. J., Chavannes, N. H., & Versluis, A. (2022).
Online synchronous focus group interviews: Practical considerations.
Qualitative Research, *23*(6), 1810–1820. https://doi.org/10.1177
/14687941221110161

Williamson, V. (2016). On the ethics of crowdsourced research. *PS:
Political Science & Politics*, *49*(1), 77–81. https://doi.org/10.1017/
S1049096515001 16X

Willis, G. (2017). Cognitive interviewing in survey design: State of the science and future directions. In D. L. Vanette & J. A. Krosnick (Eds.), *The Palgrave handbook of survey research* (pp. 103–7). SAGE.

Winseck, D. (2020). Vampire squids, 'the broken internet' and platform regulation. *Journal of Digital Media & Policy, 11*(3), 241–282. https://doi.org/10.1386/jdmp_00025_1

Woodyatt, C. R., Finneran, C. A., & Stephenson, R. (2016). In-person versus online focus group discussions: A comparative analysis of data quality. *Qualitative Health Research, 26*(6), 741–9. https://doi.org/10.1177/1049732316631510

Wu, A. X., & Taneja, H. (2021). Platform enclosure of human behavior and its measurement: Using behavioral trace data against platform episteme. *New Media & Society, 23*(9), 2650–67. https://doi.org/10.1177/1461444820933547

Yadlin-Segal, A., Tsuria, R., & Bellar, W. (2020). The ethics of studying digital contexts: Reflections from three empirical case studies. *Human Behavior and Emerging Technologies, 2*(2), 168–78. https://doi.org/10.1002/hbe2.183

Yan, W., Zhang, Y., Hu, T., & Kudva, S. (2021). How does scholarly use of academic social networking sites differ by academic discipline? A case study using ResearchGate. *Information Processing & Management, 58*(1), 102430. https://doi.org/10.1016/j.ipm.2020.102430

Youtie, J., Porter, A. L., & Huang, Y. (2017). Early social science research about big data. *Science and Public Policy, 44*(1), 65–74. https://doi.org/10.1093/scipol/scw021

Yue, S., Pilon, P., & Cavadias, G. (2002). Power of the Mann–Kendall and Spearman's rho tests for detecting monotonic trends in hydrological series. *Journal of Hydrology, 259*(1), 254–71. https://doi.org/10.1016/S0022-1694(01)00594-7

Zhou, H., & Fishbach, A. (2016). The pitfall of experimenting on the web: How unattended selective attrition leads to surprising (yet false) research conclusions. *Journal of Personality and Social Psychology, 111*(4), 493–504. https://doi.org/10.1037/pspa0000056

Zhu, J. J. H., Zhou, Y., Guan, L., Hou, L., Shen, A., & Lu, H. (2019). Applying user analytics to uses and effects of social media in China. *Asian Journal of Communication, 29*(3), 291–306, https://doi.org/10.1080/01292986.2019.1602916

Zimmer, M. (2018). Addressing conceptual gaps in big data research ethics: An application of contextual integrity. *Social Media + Society, 4*(2), 2056305118768300. https://doi.org/10.1177/2056305118768300

Zimmer, M., & Kinder-Kurlanda, K. (Eds.). (2017). *Internet research ethics for the social age: New challenges, cases, and contexts*. Peter Lang.

Zook, M., Barocas, B., boyd, d., Crawford, K., Keller, E., Gangadharan, S. P., Goodman, A., Hollander, R., Koenig, B. A., Metcalf, J., Narayanan, A., Nelson, A., & Pasquale, F. (2017). Ten simple rules for responsible big data research. *PLOS Computational Biology, 13*(3), e1005399. https://doi.org/10.1371/journal.pcbi.1005399

Zuboff, S. (2019). *The age of surveillance capitalism: The fight for a human future at the new frontier of power*. Profile Books.

INDEX